Grow Yourself a Life You'll Love

BARBARA GARRO, M.A.

Allen, Texas

Send all inquiries to:
Thomas More
An RCL Company
200 East Bethany Drive
Allen, Texas 75002-3804

BOOKSTORES:
Call Bookworld Companies 888-444-2524 or fax 941-753-9396
PARISHES AND SCHOOLS:
Thomas More Publishing 800-822-6701 or fax 800-688-8356
INTERNATIONAL:
Fax Thomas More Publishing 972-264-3719

Visit our website at www.rclweb.com

Printed in the United States of America

Library of Congress Catalog Card Number: 99-74701

ISBN 0-88347-433-6

1 2 3 4 5   03 02 01 00 99

DEDICATION

I dedicate this book to my daughters Victoria Lynne and Karen-Marie for the joys of their journeys from wee babies to wise women, and to my parents, Mildred Barbara Garro (1916-1983) and Dominic Garro (1911-1997), who loved me as much as any human parents could love a daughter. They instilled in me the glory of goodness and the greatness of a life well lived.

In addition, I want to thank professional groups, The Association for Psychological Type, The International Enneagram Association, The International Women's Writing Guild, and especially Pat Carr's Writing Groups.

A special thanks to Debra Hampton for midwifing the birth of *Grow Yourself a Life You'll Love* with empathy and professional excellence.

CONTENTS

Part Two: Planting Good Seeds in Fertile Soil

Part Three: Harvest—Uniting Body, Mind and Spirit

INTRODUCTION

When you understand why you are the way you are, you'll be kinder to yourself. When you understand others better, you'll like them more and be less critical. This will help them like you more and make your life more harmonious. Think about how much better your life would be if you got along better with the love of your life, your parents, children, siblings, other relatives, friends, co-workers, and neighbors.

You will learn that the reasons you do the things you do come from seeds planted in your nonconscious or subconscious mind from the time you were very small. These seeds or beliefs, presumptions, assumptions, and events that drive your behavior remain hidden from your conscious awareness in your subconscious mind. *Grow Yourself a Life You'll Love* motivates you to look at the seeds planted long ago to decide if they are still valid for you.

Grow Yourself a Life You'll Love is a workbook divided into three parts. The first part contains exercises to help you discover information in your subconscious mind that can explain your behavior, fears, worries, and automatic or default responses. The second part provides exercises to help you understand what makes you and those in your life do the things they do. The third part includes an exercise to get you in touch with your spirit and recognize that humans are spiritual as well as physical and mental beings.

The exercises are designed to take you back through your life to root out outdated and invalid, belief-driven programming that causes problems for you now.

Here's an invalid belief I rooted out just this year. I first learned of my shrill, loud voice at twenty-eight when my boss called me in his office to tell me that I could have been promoted to assistant to the board chairman except he couldn't stand my high-pitched voice. Off and on for thirty-five years I went to a variety of coaches to solve the problem. Each coach identified the same mechanical problem and gave me endless exercises that I practiced until my voice rasped. Not until I crept quietly into my subconscious mind did I discover the false beliefs and fears that pushed me to scream for recognition and approval. Looking back I realized that my mother, father, and brother all had low, soft voices. Until I entered the corporate world at eighteen I did, too. I started work believing that, like school, good efforts would be recognized and rewarded. Imagine the shock when I discovered the thick glass ceiling of the sixties and seventies. How could my boss tell me I did a great job as assistant credit manager, but he couldn't promote me to credit manager because the male corporate presidents wouldn't stand for a woman holding the position? So, he gave the head of accounting the credit manager's title and the new credit manager made me his assistant credit manager.

Twenty-five years later, through the same subconscious belief digging techniques you'll learn here, I consciously saw the connection between my raised voice, my fear of not being heard, and my belief that being heard would result in approval and recognition. Once my conscious mind understood my fear and the false belief that fed it, my voice volume returned to normal. And now, at fifty-six, sometimes people ask me to repeat myself because they can't hear me.

From *Grow Yourself a Life You'll Love,* you'll also gain new, exciting and useful information about the dynamics of personality, thinking styles, communication, and attitudes that make you and others act in a particular way.

Understanding reduces the pain in relationships. With fewer misunderstandings, you'll have increased quality time together, more laughs, and greater happiness than you've ever known.

You deserve happiness. Believe that with all your heart and soul. If you're not happy, you owe it to yourself to do whatever it takes to bring more happiness into your life. If your life is a dead life walking, this may sound impossible to you. But I want you to know that I believe you can do it. And somewhere inside you believe it, too, or you wouldn't be reading this book.

It's never too late to live happily ever after. Other people have happy lives. You can, too, once you lighten your load of anger, fear, worry, envy, jealousy, hate, insecurity, and depression.

I encourage you to do the inner work exercises, locating and pulling out the weeds that choke the happiness out of your life. See false personality for what it is, the lies you tell yourself and the secrets you keep from others. Learn what triggers anger, violence, passive aggression, procrastination, and depression in yourself and others.

Then discover your unique and wonderful personality that works beautifully for you once you understand it. After you understand yourself, understanding others follows in natural progression. With understanding comes forgiveness. Once you can forgive, you are freed from the need to judge. With the capacity of forgiveness and non-judgment comes true unconditional love and an understanding of God's love for you. The last chapter speaks to coming full circle by embracing your spiritual self.

Let *Grow Yourself a Life You'll Love* help you push out of your boxes, climb over your fences and live, really live, a life you'll love. You deserve a life you'll love living, and I hope with all my heart and soul that you never stop trying new things until you have it.

HOW TO USE THIS BOOK

When you watch in amazement people who seem to live charmed, wonderful lives, your negative response says, "They were born lucky and I wasn't." The positive response says, "If they can cultivate a good life, so can I, as soon as I learn what's different about the way we each make decisions in our lives."

Grow Yourself a Life You'll Love can help you make positive, self-affirming decisions. You can begin by choosing from among the suggested ways to use this book:

1. Begin by doing all the exercises cold; then read the chapters.
2. Follow me through the book chronologically and do each exercise.
3. Zero in on the chapters that speak to you in the order that seems right.
4. Use the book as a problem-solver reference.
5. Read the book with a significant person in your life, sharing the exercises and discussing the concepts.

The plan of the book solidly focuses you to *Grow Yourself a Life You'll Love* beginning with the first exercise to set three personal and three business or service goals that would make your life better.

Each chapter then creates a unique environment for you to do the exercises, stop to think about the ideas, and take them in. This inner "digging-learning-doing with confidence" format changed the course of my life. I share these ideas with the hope that your life will be made better, too, when you use them.

I based this book on knowledge, skills, attitudes, and self-reflection that helped me create my current life, a life I love living. Three sections are presented to create what good life means for you. Part One shows you what causes problems. Part Two shows you what you have to know and do to create harmonious relationships. Part Three guides you to connect with your spiritual self, a missing branch for many people, to create a life you'll love living.

Throughout the chapters you will find acronyms and other techniques to help you remember concepts and cultivate your new knowledge. You'll feel terrific the first time you understand the thinking system a speaker is using. It's fun to train with TV sitcoms and talk shows.

Dig in. I've spent my first fifty-six years figuring out the how-to's of creating a happy life. Like many others, much of my relationship thinking was just plain wrong for years. For example, I discovered it is loving rather than selfish to set limits and boundaries, because nobody benefited when I let people walk all over me. Coming out from behind my false personality mask scared me. Perennial change challenged me. Transplanted ideas were hard to root, and I wondered if my new good habits would ever bear fruit. One by stubborn one, though, each bad habit got dug out and replaced by a better habit, sometimes with free choice and out of the habit rut altogether. And, I even lost that last ten pounds, but that's another book.

Play with the concepts presented. Try out the suggestions. See if you find yourself less stressed. Do before and after comparisons to learn if these concepts help you get along better with the people in your life. Make habits out of the ideas that work for you. Along the way, discover new things about yourself. Like any banquet, take what appeals, leave what doesn't.

I wish you joy on your journey.

PART ONE

Destroying the Weeds That Spoil Your Life

Consider moving yourself to a new level of reality where you recognize that every choice you make affects your life. The concept is as simple as *Good choices grow good lives* and *bad choices grow bad lives* and as complex as *How do I know the difference?* So Part One helps you begin by looking at choices that suck the juice out of your life—keeping secrets, telling lies, and fueling angers that escalate out of control. The push-pull of holding back and letting off steam keeps your life thin and weak, instead of full and rich. By understanding the root causes of emotional pressures, you are better able to gain control. Control enables you to maintain a calm core that gives you confidence to communicate authentically, face and solve your personal and business problems, and gain life satisfaction you never dreamed possible.

You really do have choice, no matter how bleak your situation. And we all get to bleak at some points in our lives. That's one way life challenges us to new growth. Exercising your power of choice gives greater dimension, meaning, and purpose to your life.

Chapter 1

Introduction

Yesterday is fruit eaten, a bloom spent; tomorrow is only a possibility; and today, only today, is in full bloom—so pick and enjoy today's fruits and blossoms.

Did you ever wonder, sweat dripping from your chin, hands crusted with dirt, where weeds come from? No one plants them. You couldn't buy weed seeds if you wanted them. Yet, without back-breaking labor, they aggressively take over your yard.

Old biases are like those weeds. They lay buried deep in your subconscious and they can take over your everyday life. Old biases come from yesterdays that are no more. One of mine involved making money. I never wanted to make more than I needed. When I processed the origin of the belief, I discovered that it came from my mother during my teen years. My father burned with a passion to wheel and deal. One day he came home with a contract between my parents and a consortium of investors to purchase and develop the first casino in Atlantic City, New Jersey. Around the dinner table, my brother and I listened as my father explained his plans to my mother.

What she said bored deep into my young, fertile mind, "I'm not signing it. If you get into that, I'll never see you. You'll be all involved in your wheeling and dealing making money we don't need. What do you want all that money for anyway? The more money you have, the more people connive to get it. You do what you want, but I'm not signing your paper." He didn't do it. Some months later the property sold for $14 million. And I had a limiting belief that said making too much money was a bad thing to do. After I processed the belief that held me back financially, I doubled my salary, bought a house, and started a nest egg.

Think of yesterday's biases as pushing your automatic pilot button and manual piloting as thinking in the now. Author and psychologist David J. Lieberman says that the more automated our lives are the wider the gap between reality and our perception of reality, moving us further into our own little world.

An African proverb tells us: *If there is no enemy within, the enemy outside can do us no harm.*

Look at the biases behind your need to keep secrets, tell and believe lies, and make assumptions and presumptions. Do you keep your anger a secret because you are afraid if anyone saw your temper they wouldn't want to be around you any more? Do you tell yourself it is okay to take office supplies home because you work extra hours and you don't get paid for them? Do you assume men will behave one way and women another? Do you presume that your friend will let you use the car when you visit? Secrets, lies, assumptions, and presumptions are unilateral decisions you make without the courtesy of checking with others involved.

Worse, they are all blind spots in our personalities, reasons behind our actions that we need to see but don't, can't, or won't. While some blind spots function as numbing or denial, some fall outside of our knowing on any level. Hybrids of blind spots grow into full-blown illusions. Every day people convince themselves to believe what they want to be true, instead of the truth that those in their lives know is reality. The abused who believes a violent person's promise that the hitting won't happen again. Liars who think their lies make truth the lie. Drug addicts who blame the drugs for their bad behavior rather than themselves who chose to take the drugs.

From the Talmud we are told that we do not see things as they are. We see them as we are.

Secrets & Lies—Thorns that Bite

Most of us plain confound others by acting one way in public and another in private. Each of us is like a cast of characters: Who's on stage? Who's back stage? Who's hiding behind the curtain afraid to come out? If this begins to sound like the stuff of novels, remember fictional characters are exaggerated personalities.

My mom would say, "Oh what a tangled web we weave when first we practice to deceive." Secrets and lies destroy intimacy, build walls between you and those who care about you. Openness and honesty draw people to you.

Think about what you discovered doing the exercise on this page to check out the secrets in your life. How many family and personal secrets could you list? When you examined your strongest biases, how many still

Secrets & Lies Exercise

For this exercise, go back through your family and personal history and check out these areas for hidden secrets and lies:

- *Family secrets*
- *Personal secrets*

Examine your strong biases to learn which are really yours and which are leftovers from relatives and others. Put each category at the top of a letter-size sheet and start ruminating in your mind. Be patient, thoughts will come to you. Just take a few deep breaths, relax and let the process take over. Allow at least 30 minutes to complete the exercise. And save those sheets, because you will be surprised how many secrets and lies come to you over the course of the next several days. Add them to the sheets. The more you can come up with, the more sense you'll be able to make out of things that happened in your life. Take a break now and complete the exercise before you read further.

worked for you? How many turned out to be things you believed that really weren't so for you anymore?

If you haven't completed the exercise yet, why not take a break and do it now? You want to foster a detective mentality about your biases, the attitudes that come from those biases, the emotions that come from those attitudes, and the actions you take based on your motivating emotions. This work teaches you interesting things about yourself. You may want to list those particular things that surprised you the most.

You can't be yourself unless you know who you are. You can't know who you are unless you know the reasons behind your self-destructive behaviors. The way to find the reasons behind self-destructive behaviors is to take yourself inside to the source of your biases and fears.

What you don't know and what you know that isn't so can hurt you, spoil your relationships, and may ruin your whole life. Carl Jung said that to confront a person with his own shadow is to show him his own light. Your shadow side is the person you become when you believe no one important is watching you.

How good we are at fooling ourselves and others! How hard we work to keep people from finding out our secrets! And we lie. I was eavesdropping one day, as writers are wont to do, and I heard someone ask this question, "Do you want me to give you my honest answer or do you want me to give you the answer so I don't have to sleep with one eye open?"

Why can't we just be honest with ourselves and others? *I am fat because I eat too much. I am not getting my work done because of plain laziness. My marriage is rocky because I'm too self-centered.* When we face the reality of our problems, we see the fault in our behavior. Wrong behavior must be changed. Change is hard. It's easier to lie to ourselves and blame others.

Psychiatrist Sigmund Freud called this practice of hiding what we can't or won't deal with *repression.* Emotions we repress, suppress, or flat out deny don't disappear; they live inside our subconscious mind where they wreak havoc on us mentally and physically.

Addictions, for example, are often secrets made up of what we desire as well as what we purposely avoid. Not only addictions, but also expectations and entitlements are secrets, as well. How can you recognize yours? Present-moment detective work. When you are alert to the here and now, you notice your cravings, how anxious you get when they aren't fulfilled, and what you do to retaliate against a world that refuses to satisfy you.

Awareness puts us in control of our circumstances so we can consciously control ourselves and our environment to the best of our abilities. Awareness comes from living in the now and examining old programming to see if it's still valid for us today.

Move back through your life and look for answers. Suppose you have a deathly fear of dogs and don't know why. Ask family members if they might know why. A friend's girlfriend in her fifties froze in her tracks as soon as she saw a dog. One evening at a family reunion, he told relatives of Vicky's paranoid fear of dogs. Well no sooner had his mouth closed, did her Aunt Billie say, "Sure she'd be afraid of dogs seeing as how that stray attacked her playing in her little sandbox. He clawed her pretty good until her daddy took the pitchfork to him." Vicky had forgotten all about that attack as a toddler, but her belief that strange dogs hurt you stayed rooted deep in her mind. Now that Vicky understands the origin of her fear, she no longer allows her automatic pilot to trigger an emotional attack when she sees a dog. She has taken over conscious control of her reaction to dogs.

You've probably suspected this whole secrets and lies thing can really wreak havoc in your relationships. And you're right.

Here's how secrets and lies operate in our daily lives. They become masks of false personality. You probably don't like the sound of that term, but it may be easier to stomach if you think of false personality as a bad habit. Truth be told, you don't like the sound of any other bad habit either. Bad habits have lots of ugly names: addictions, compulsions, dysfunctional patterns, obsessions, and can escalate out of control to mental illnesses like obsessive-compulsive disorders where people are driven to wash their hands literally dozens of times a day.

If it makes you feel any better, I hated raking through my life and digging out my own secrets and lies. Please hear me out, open minded to the end of the concept of false personality before you form your conclusions.

False personality operates out of our unconscious mind in a habitual, machine-like way that takes away our opportunity to make present-moment choices. This automatic behavior pattern of the false personality damages our relationships. An example: You want to get dressed up Saturday and go to a nice restaurant. Your friend wants to go casual to a Chinese buffet. Your words agree to go to the Chinese buffet, but your voice sounds sharp and the timbre has angry undertones. You suffer through the dinner and your friend is also not likely to have a good time with accommodating but suffering you. Your friend probably won't be anxious to have dinner with you any time soon. Wouldn't it have been better to speak up instead of spoiling the dinner, creating a situation where neither of you could enjoy the dinner?

Most people make these dumb choices to avoid conflict. Using false personality masks may seem like an easy way to keep the peace. But whose peace? Certainly not yours, with all the churning and resentment going on inside.

Wearing false personality masks begins early on. We are babies born of imperfect parents into an imperfect world. Our imperfect world gives us error messages from the time we are very little—*Don't do that. Don't cry. Don't be loud. I don't like you when you get angry.*

We learn that what we instinctively do in some situations is not okay. So to survive, we learn to cover up our way with what is okay so we can get along in our environment. In this way we begin very early pandering to the more powerful. We spend a lot of energy squelching our natural inclinations and trying to figure out what our little corner of the world wants from us. Through positive and negative feedback, we form habits or patterns. We then become a product, if you will, of our environment.

We learn to survive in our environment and little by little we forget who the real person of me really is. Our carefully crafted false personality takes over our lives and, except for a glimmer or two here and there, we then come to believe that this false personality driving us is really our true self. This person you made up to survive in your environment thus becomes you, or more accurately, the person you and everybody else believes is you.

The get-along false personality, unfortunately, has one nearly fatal flaw—it cannot find your happiness. As long as it stands a tall, thick wall between your true self and your waiting possibilities, it blocks your only door to happiness, which is you acting as your true self, your authentic self.

So many times we lose our authentic selves by denying our feelings to the point where the wall of false personality gets so thick the feelings don't even seep through any more. We act like we are intellectually above feelings and emotionality, seeing them as weakness or vulnerability. So our feelings get buried in a black hole of denial and we become partial people, the false personality part that tells you, "You're not okay but it's our secret."

Look at yourself as a garden plot. Your caregivers keep testing your soil. Too much crying. Take crying out. Put in waiting. Too much anger. Take that out. Put in obedience. By the time you are 10, if you have generally been a good child, you've repressed certain parts of your authentic self because your caregivers told you it wasn't any good. And you learned to wear your false masks to please them. Sometimes they were right and sometimes they weren't. Often, the playful, risk-taking, fun-loving, curious characteristics are the ones we lose to make ourselves acceptable in others' eyes. Now it is up to you to go back and reclaim your authentic self and throw away the unhealthy false personality masks that are confusing you and everybody else.

Mahatma Gandhi said, "A 'no' uttered from the deepest conviction is better than a 'yes' merely uttered to please, or what is worse, to avoid trouble."

Recognize first that you can't control what you aren't aware of. Your present-moment detective work becomes key to a better understanding of who you are and why you do the things you do. Truthfully, now, haven't you been curious to understand why some events in your life turned out the way they did?

Let's start satisfying your curiosity about yourself. You probably suspected, and again you're right, that false personality is a big subject, in fact, the subject of whole books. Here the aim is working knowledge so you can discover and discard your masks of false personality and return to your authentic self, free of the need to hide your true self ever again. (I interject a clarification to avoid anyone confusing the term false personality with the psychological disorder multiple personalities. False personality is learned behavior, a habit we can unlearn, or break. Multiple personality is a mental disorder where one person has two or more distinct personalities, often completely unknown to one another, each of which dominates at different times, such as the situation with the fictional "Dr. Jekyll & Mr. Hyde.")

By definition false personality consists of situational masks we wear to fool others into believing we feel or think one way when, in fact, our thinking may be exactly the opposite. False personality unfortunately leaves us running on emotional and spiritual empty. On the one hand, it's not who we are and people know it on some level, so their instincts tell them we don't make sense, and they avoid intimacy with us. On the other, we can become what we pretend to be—so we must be very careful about what we pretend to be.

Author Brian D. Biro in *Beyond Success* says, "No one can be loved until they let themselves be seen. No one can be seen until they learn to love themselves."

Here are some of the faces I wrote down when I did the exercise:

- ❖ Brave Face
- ❖ Competent Face
- ❖ In Control Face
- ❖ Smart Face
- ❖ Not Shocked Face
- ❖ Not Angry Face
- ❖ Interested Face

At one time or another most of us have used false personality masks to hide suppressed fear and anger. You know those brave faces and those smiling faces we wear when inside we are scared to death or fuming. When completing the first exercise, you may have discovered, like I did, you wear these faces sometimes. As you probably suspected, false personality consists of a variety of masks we wear in a variety of situations.

Still we wear false personality masks because we believe they help us in our relationships. They hide grief, hate, rage, fear, shame, and guilt. Who wants these terrible emotions hanging out for everyone to see? Indeed, those of you who hate your bosses probably better not let them know it. However, if you always seem to go along with what others want to do, wouldn't you like to know that need that keeps you from speaking up?

Need is the root cause of false personality masks—need for approval, need for security, need for power. *I can't tell you how I really feel, because then you won't like me. I go along with what you want because I am afraid you will leave me. I bully people because I am insecure but I don't want anyone to see my weakness.* The need for approval says, "I am only okay if the world likes me." The need for security says, "I am afraid for my well-being and I am forced to do these things to survive." The need for power says, "My need for control forces me to dominate you."

Your Many Faces Exercise

Here's what jazz musician, Charlie Parker, had to say about being authentic: "If you ain't lived it, it ain't going to come out of your horn." The truth is false personality masks don't feel good on the inside and they don't play particularly well on the outside, either. People who know you can tell when you are hiding something. They may not know exactly what, but they find it hard to buy what your face is selling.

For this exercise, go back over the last thirty days. This information is just for you, so be honest with yourself. Like before, answer each of these questions on a separate sheet.

As you can see, masks are lies that hide the truth of who you are, therefore, block your personal growth, and leave you behind a wall where no one can get close to you.

Fyodor Dostoevsky in *The Brothers Karamazov* wrote: *Above all, don't lie to yourself. The man who lies to himself and listens to his own lie comes to such a pass that he cannot distinguish the truth within him, or around him, and so loses all respect for himself and for others. And having no respect he ceases to love, and in order to occupy and distract himself without love he gives way to passions and coarse pleasures, and sinks to bestiality in his vices, all from continual lying to other men and to himself. . . .*

Dostoevsky's worst-case scenario sounds a powerful wake-up call. Do the inner work to root out your secrets and lies so you understand why you do the things you do. This makes positive change possible, and such positive change grows the life you'll love living.

Remember to stay alert to the crops of assumptions and presumptions you plant in other people's gardens without their permission.

Hopefully, you've scratched, dug, uprooted, and planted some new ideas. To help refresh you memory as time goes by, here is your harvest summary for Secrets & Lies—Thorns That Bite:

Four Main Points

1. Expose your secrets and lies as the relationship killers they are.

2. Your biases determine your attitudes, which determine your feelings, which drive your actions.

3. When you choose to live in the present moment, change is possible, and positive change grows you a life you'll love living.

4. Yesterday is fruit eaten, a bloom spent; tomorrow is only a possibility; and today, only today, is in full bloom—so pick and enjoy today's fruits and blossoms.

How many faces do you wear?

What makes you afraid to say what you really think and feel?

What people make you afraid to be yourself?

What situations make you afraid to be yourself?

What secret thoughts and feelings are you afraid of letting loose into the world?

Take a break now and complete the exercise before you read further.

PLEASE HEAR WHAT I'M NOT SAYING

(Don't Be Fooled)

Don't be fooled by me. Don't be fooled by the mask I wear. For I wear a mask, I wear a thousand masks, masks that I'm afraid to take off, and none of them is me. Pretending is an art that is second nature with me, but don't be fooled.

I give the impression that I'm secure, that all is sunny and unruffled with me, within as well as without; that confidence is my name and coolness is my game; that the waters are calm and I'm in command and I need no one. But don't believe it; please don't.

My surface may seem smooth, but my surface is my mask, my ever-varying and ever-concealing mask. Beneath lies no smugness, no coolness, no complacence. Beneath dwells the real me, in confusion, in fear, in loneliness. But I hide this; I don't want anybody to know it. I panic at the thought of my weakness being exposed. That's why I frantically create a mask to hide behind, a nonchalant sophisticated facade to help me pretend, to shield me from the glance that knows. But such a glance is precisely my salvation. My only salvation. And I know it. It's the only thing that can liberate me from myself, from my own self-built prison walls, from the barriers I so painstakingly erect. But I don't tell you this. I don't dare. I'm afraid to.

I'm afraid your glance will not be followed by love and acceptance. I'm afraid that you will think less of me, that you'll laugh, and your laugh will kill me. I'm afraid that deep down inside I'm nothing, that I'm just no good, and that you'll see and reject me. So I play my games, my desperate, pretending games, with a façade of assurance on the outside and a trembling child within. And so begins the parade of masks, the glittering but empty parade of masks. And my life becomes a front.

I idly chatter with you in the suave tones of surface talk. I tell you everything that's really nothing, nothing of what's crying within me. So when I'm going through my routine, don't be fooled by what I'm saying. Please listen carefully and try to hear what I'm NOT saying; what I'd like to be able to say; what, for survival, I need to say but can't say. I dislike the hiding. Honestly I do. I dislike the superficial phony games I'm playing.

I'd really like to be genuine, spontaneous, and me; but you have to help me. You have to help me by holding out your hand, even when that's the last thing that I seem to want or need. Each time you are kind and gentle and encouraging, each time you try to understand because you really care, my heart begins to grow wings. Very small wings. Very feeble wings. But wings. With your sensitivity and sympathy and your power of understanding, I can make it. You can breathe life into me. It will not be easy for you. A long conviction of worthlessness builds strong walls. But love is stronger than strong walls, and therein lies my hope. Please try to beat down those walls with firm hands, but with gentle hands, for a child is very sensitive, and I AM a child.

Who am I, you may wonder? I am someone you know very well. For I am every man, every woman, every child . . . every human you meet.

Anonymous

WATER AND FERTILIZE NEW GROWTH BY . . .

- Keeping up the detective work you started on secrets and lies by adding to your sheets.
- Keeping up the detective work you started on your many faces by adding to your list.
- Keep working on present moment focus and avoid getting stuck in yesterday or tomorrow.

Assumptions and Presumptions—Weeds We Harvest as Fruit

I define assumption as an unproven, unsupportable guess about someone or something. There are two kinds: assumptions about what others think of us and assumptions about what we think others are thinking and feeling. Of course assuming is arrogant—when anyone thinks they know how someone else feels, thinks, would react, instead of allowing that person to speak his or her own thoughts and feelings. Of course, we all do it.

Assumptions and perceptions come from past experience. The first time I went to an Indian restaurant, nothing pleased me. The bread was soggy and tasteless; the dipping sauces were strangely spiced; the dessert menu was horrid, and the restaurant smelled rancid. No one would have been able to talk me into going into another Indian restaurant, except in one occasion that I was in Manhattan with a group of about a dozen women, and they all wanted to go to an Indian restaurant. It smelled terrific; the bread was to-die-for; everything I tasted was better than the last thing; and the dessert menu was marvelous. Yet without a forced circumstance, I probably would have maintained my closed mind about Indian food based on one past experience.

That's the point. Assumptions close your mind to reality. They are absolutely arrogant. They steal from people their right and freedom to express themselves. They are the opposite of an accepting attitude which allows people to answer for themselves. The accepting approach is a camcorder approach, knowing only what you actually see and hear. The camcorder approach requires an amazing discipline, and people will love you for it.

You may be thinking: Wait just a minute, if I take this camcorder approach what about all I learned from past experience; do I just forget about it? The answer is yes and no. Prior knowledge and expectations are important. They help determine our perceptions.

For example, prior experience tells us that soup can be burning hot. So while we expect soup to be a hot food, our perception tells us to be cautious and check out the temperature so we don't burn our mouths.

Keep uppermost in your mind this working knowledge of the thinking system. While the boundaries between sensation and perception can blur, generally, perception interprets sensation from simple stimuli, giving stimuli meaning and also organization. The next mental process after perception is cognition, more complex, and involving receiving, storing, retrieving, and making use of our knowledge. The reason I describe this process is because when we assume and presume, we fail to move to that important next step, cognition, where we get the chance to make intelligent judgments about information. Remember, learning results from confusion.

When we fail to move from perception to cognition, we put a filter between ourselves and reality. When we then behave out of assumptions and presumptions, we deserve the poor results we get.

If we think all bosses are jerks, we are more likely to take the boss' behavior personally. If we think about our generic boss assumption, logic tells us it can't be true, but we often refuse to use logic in our assumptions, presumptions, prejudices, and biases, both good and bad.

I once facilitated a Parents Without Partners program for single parents about how assumptions and presumptions wreak havoc during the getting-to-know-you stage of dating. I took a poll asking two questions: *Are the people you meet dating a treasure chest of delights?* Or: *Are the people you meet dating a Pandora's box of horrors?* When the room revealed practically a dead heat, I decided to get more information anonymously. During a break I asked people to write one word on a slip of paper that described dates as treasure chests or horrors. Look at a sampling of their one-word descriptions:

Assumptions & Presumptions Exercise

For this exercise, fill in the blanks in the list below

Men are ___________

Women are _________

Children are _________

The world is _________

Life is _____________

Sex is _____________

People are __________

Bosses are __________

Money is ___________

Treasure Chest	**Horrors**
Affable	Bitter Bad-mouthers
Lovable	Unlovable
Tender	Alley Cats
Sensitive	Avengers
Adventurous	Disease carriers
Charming	Crazies
Comforting	Cry-babies
Interesting	Pigs
Generous	Selfish takers

Assumptions and presumptive guesses are never bull's eyes. Your point of view is only 100 percent accurate when it relates to you personally. Consider new gardeners choosing plants for the shady side and the sunny side of their homes. Would they guess whether to put a plant in the shade or sun by looking at it? Unlikely. Most would ask the seller or look at the care instructions for each plant. So what makes so many people assume and presume all over the place about how to care for the people in their lives?

Presumptions can hurt people deeply. When I was a high school freshman, my English nun, who had told me I was a writer, forced me to skip lunch one day, sit in homeroom, and write a poem. She said she wanted to see if I also had a talent for writing poetry. She gave me a 40-minute window to write a poem, when I was hungry and annoyed about being made to skip lunch. When she read the poem, she said, "Okay, you can't write poetry." Twenty-six poetry-less years later, when my mother died, my grief burst out of me in a poem that was published in our local paper. Over the years many of my poems have been published.

Choosing to examine the things we make up about life and people takes a strong character. Most of us have held on to our mental tattoos of thought for longer than we can easily remember. Some of our mental tattoos are global. For example, some people believe their world is friendly, and others believe it is hostile. In reality, the world is, at any given time, what people make it. Change means reframing your automatic reactions by examining your biases, the attitudes they create, and the feelings attitudes create, so you can change your automatic reactions. *Metanoia* is a Greek word for this emotional process, and it translates into change of attitude, change of heart.

Let people teach you who they are. Learn to stop seeing people through your opinions and let them show themselves to you. Stop cheating yourself and others by making assumptions supported by untested perceptions. When you hear with your filters, you aren't listening for the real meaning behind the words others say. The messages you get are distorted.

Practice some of these conversational listening skills:

- ❖ Maintain eye contact and discipline yourself against distraction.
- ❖ Maintain an open and accepting attitude.
- ❖ Turn your talking off—Solomon (18:13) said, "He who answers before listening, that is his folly and his shame."
- ❖ Turn your judgment off, and turn your full attention to the person or people you are with.

- ❖ Listen between the lines and look for incidents when the facial expressions and tone of voice fail to match the words said.
- ❖ Gain more information by using these two magic phrases: *Tell me more!* and *What is it you would like me to do now?*
- ❖ Avoid drawing premature conclusions and aim your focus on the speaker's message.
- ❖ Respond only occasionally both to show interest and to reflect back empathetically that you really understand the meaning the speaker intends to convey.

Over lunch with a married woman in my writing group, we had this conversation:

> **She:** I have to tell you I am really jealous of your freedom. You get to do whatever you want, come and go as you please.
>
> **Me:** And I have to tell you that I hate it when anyone tells me they are jealous of me because jealously is such a horrible emotion.
>
> **She:** Oh, that's silly, I didn't mean anything by it. Actually I meant it as a compliment.
>
> **Me:** Hear me, jealously is a mean emotion and I don't like it when people say they are jealous of me. Besides, I am not single because I don't want to be married.
>
> **She:** Oh, you're too independent to be married. No man would marry a woman as independent as you.
>
> **Me:** That's a horrible thing to say.
>
> **She:** I'm sorry. I thought you knew.

I disagreed, however, I understood that this woman thought I was unmarryable. Then, I remembered what my father had said a few years before he died, "Babe, you're too independent to be married."

Listening to others gives us information about how we are presenting to the world positively or negatively.

Think about the truth of this statement: We can't totally know ourselves unless we listen to other people. What do people say about you? What do you learn when you disagree?

My hope is you've become more aware of your own assumptions, presumptions, and perceptions. To help you remember to keep on pulling these communication choking weeks, here is your harvest summary for Assumptions & Presumptions, Weeds We Harvest as Fruit.

Three Main Points

1. Avoid assuming the right to make up in your head what thoughts are in the heads and what feelings are in the hearts of other people.
2. Use a camcorder approach in your interactions with people and ask what people are thinking and feeling, listening with 100 percent of your attention to what they are willing to tell you.
3. Practice good conversational listening skills and be willing to do the hard work of attentive listening.

Water and Fertilize New Growth by . . .

❖ Keep finding and examining your generic labels like those in the assumptions and presumptions exercise above.

❖ Spend a day in 100 percent camcorder mode, assuming nothing you can't see or hear.

❖ Start and keep a list of every time you hear people say something from their perception of the way you are.

We've concentrated on stinking thinking in this chapter. Next, we move on to emotions that harden hearts.

Chapter 2

Drought — Emotions that Harden Hearts

Introduction

Lack of love is drought. Frustration, resentment, fear, and anger harden hearts and make anyone hard to love. Understand one basic truth: You can't be angry and happy at the same time. So if happiness is what you want, you need to stop holding on to anger.

For those with little short fuses, that means removing your stock of fuel and gaining control of your emotions to avoid blow-ups.

For the long-suffering, that means processing out anger you have been storing for years and years. Every time you didn't speak up but wanted to. Every time you stuffed your feelings down because you wanted to keep peace. Every time you kept quiet because you felt speaking made things worse. Each one of those times sits someplace inside you, eating at you from some level.

Anger, like termite infestation, never stops destroying your peace of mind. That means anger keeps you from being able to fully enjoy the good times. Remembering the bad times gets in the way.

You love someone, yet you feel jealous, so you turn on your loved one in anger. What causes the jealousy? Look for causes relating more to your insecurity in the relationship and lack of trust than anything your loved one actually did.

Judgmental egos need to be right and self-righteously proclaim other people's wrongs. You have only to catch the news to see we live in a fear-based society driven to point out what's wrong.

An arrogant seeker once challenged a Zen master to explain the concept of heaven. But the master told him he was someone who was asleep in the dark and he would not waste his time with him.

The seeker exploded in anger, raised his sword, and said, "I could kill you for your arrogance."

"That," said the master, is "hell!"

When the seeker saw the truth of the master's words, he replaced his sword in its sheath, bowed, and thanked the master for his truth.

"That," said the master, "is heaven."

Did the master make the seeker angry, or did anger course through the seeker's mind like the blood in the seeker's veins?

All of us come face to face with anger. Keep a focus on understanding anger and dealing with it so it can't fester inside you and rot your life. When you understand anger and violence dynamics, seek the causes of your own anger, and manage conflict well enough, you can keep and improve your important relationships.

Kudzu, the aggressive vine that grows in the Southern states of the United States, destroys the trees it grows on. In the context of *No one is an island and we thrive as humans by growing up others,* we are social beings. For most people, true independence rarely happens.

Relationships are interdevelopmental, interdependent, and dependent. So an ongoing life question becomes, "Do we kill the trees we grow on or do we serve them?"

Recognize that anger and violence serve neither the perpetrator nor the victim. Remember: He who angers you controls you. Emotions drive actions. Acting out of uncontrolled emotions causes people to alienate others with their knee-jerk reactions.

I wish I could promise that once you learn anger and conflict management you will always have harmonious interactions. Here's an example of knowing all the skills and screwing up royally. I ordered in July fold-over business cards for the International Coach Federation's annual convention in Scottsdale, Arizona, coming up that September. I followed up regularly. Still, the week of the convention I found myself with 500 business cards out of an order of 5,000 with copy not centered on the card, a score that didn't produce an even fold, cheap paper stock which caused my photo to easily scratch, unreadable white lettering on silver, and light, broken print throughout. A friend in the quick printing business told me in printing language all the problems with the cards to arm me for my upcoming conversation with the printer. When the printer refused to acknowledge any of the problems, I found myself going on and on about the same problems . . . perseveringly. The printer stated his job was within printing quality parameters . . . perseveringly. I even offered to pay another printer and provide camera-ready copy if he would just reprint the cards right. When he said he didn't think he could please me, I asked for my up-front deposit. He countered with I owed him for the whole job. That's when I lost it. When he hung up without ending the conversation, I had time to notice the fire inside my belly that burned straight out the top of my head. For me, terms like burning mad, hot under the collar, hotter than a fire cracker, and cool down are literal. While it had been a long time since I had lost control, I saw clearly the fine line between communication guru and donkey's butt.

I had let my need to be right take precedence over my desire to work with the printer to get quality cards reprinted. During cool-down, I watered my anger with attitude adjustments, problem-solving, deep breaths, and a walk with the dog. What an uphill battle I had getting myself calmed down enough to do my work! First I called my printer friend and told her what the printer had said. She provided an empathetic ear, clear options, and positive advice—Go to the convention. When you come back, you'll decide about getting your coaching cards printed. After our conversation, I knew I had to get this monkey off my back before I could do my work. An instant action plan accomplished that: I called my printer's camera-ready art person and gave her the information she needed to provide art for an as-yet unknown printer; I walked up to City Hall and filed a Small Claim against the printer; and I decided not to tell the person who recommended the printer about the problem. The anger subsided, the problem resolved for the moment, real work became possible—for a while. Seven hours later, while making a photocopy, I found I had left an enlargement of the printer's card in the machine. It stated his proud member status in an international printing association. That quick, I got the number and called the president, who, amazingly, answered the telephone. I told him my story, asked for his help, which he offered, and faxed him the pertinent information. Again, I could produce work.

As you can see, my virtue against anger is fragile, at best. Be gentle with yourself, recognize knowing the right things to do in a situation doesn't mean your emotions will allow you to do them.

Most of us have a few anger triggers. Not getting high quality work can set me off every time. Why? My expectation says: When I am paying someone good money, I expect them to give me good work for it. Reality says that Barbara Garro doesn't live in a perfect world and mistakes will happen on the jobs people do for her. Now, I bridge my expectation with reality quite well intellectually, and, as you can see, less well emotionally. Although I keep getting better at this bridge thing all the time.

Be truthful with yourself, as well. Look at how easily anger comes out of you and what triggers it. Is it a need for approval, a desire for control, or a security issue?

Remember also the seeker in the story and ask yourself how much anger you are holding inside. Why didn't you? You should have. You never think of me. I always have to give in. You always get what you want. I never get what I want.

Edna St. Vincent Millay's comment about personal problems serves as a wake-up call. *It is not true that life is one damn thing after another—it's one damned thing over and over.*

Resentments build, sometimes for years, even whole generations. Resentment is like a seasoned wood pile. Give it a spark of annoyance, and it fuels a bonfire of anger. Easy anger comes from resentments you feel about the way others, society, and your environment treat you. Few can hide resentment. Others think: There's an angry one, because resentment seeps into voices and colors the peace-promoting words. Look, I'm not angry . . . nothing is wrong . . . let's forget about this and go and have a good time, all said with tight jaws and clenched teeth.

In addition, resentment sneaks out in active or passive resistance. Active resistance explodes in anger and violence, and passive resistance implodes in procrastination and depression. Both actions of emotional backlash dig furrows of hurt and harden hearts as they erode trust and water fears.

At the bottom of the resentment lies a fear of not getting what we want. That makes us feel frustrated, and frustration can lead to conflict. Conflict says, *If you get what you want, I can't get what I want.*

Add to the frustration compost pot that people rarely want the same things at the same times, and you see how relationships produce conflict. Going out for dessert, you want Italian coffee and I want ice cream. Probably we can resolve the disagreement without anger. If not, then our dessert disagreement can escalate: frustration, anger, disagreement, to full-blown conflict, ire, rage, where loss of control moves the angry emotions into violence. Out-of-control anger turns into rage and then fury, the destructive rage commonly called violence in our society.

If you're thinking: Wait a minute, a dessert disagreement leading to violence, I don't think so. My children still speak about the time we came home happy from picking chestnuts we planned to roast and eat. Their father flew into an instant rage claiming they were poison. Our fun activity ended in tears and unhappy memories.

Emotional reactions come ten times faster than cognitive reactions. The angry react before they take time to think. Frustrated, angry people teeter on the outer edge of emotional control. With their anger easily triggered, they make being with them horrid at times. Ironically, neither the angry nor the depressed can easily reconstruct the scenario of how they came to the states they live in.

Stored anger, like fermenting corn in a silo, remains potentially explosive. Even the depressed, who usually don't hurt others physically, can become active aggressors at any time. You don't want to be around when a long-suffering imploder explodes.

You may wonder why so many angry and violent people appear to get away with their abominable behavior. Passive people, trying to keep the peace, help them, make excuses for them, blame themselves for the behavior that triggered the angry outburst, and work hard to keep the nut case from going back over the edge. *Oh, don't pay any attention to Rantin' Rave. Just ignore Nitpicky. Look, I'll be right back—it's easier if I just give Screamy what she wants. I have to take the good with the bad. Beatin' Bob brings home a good paycheck every week and we live pretty well. He loves me in his own way. Every once in a while he takes his frustrations out on me. He always says he's sorry.*

Still, passive people control their own anger at a dear emotional price. The fire that burns within distracts their minds and procrastination happens. Sometimes they turn their fury onto themselves in blame and guilt for the angry situations in their lives and get depressed.

Heed a Biblical warning: Make no friendship with an angry. . . [one], and with a furious . . . [one] do not go. (Proverbs 22:24)

The warning works, however, only when you have choice. When the volatile one is a parent, child, sibling or other relative, you need skills to protect yourself from their angry outbursts. So, learning anger processing and conflict management become incredibly useful skills for your overall mental, physical, and spiritual well-being, because no one can totally escape anger.

Sometimes when you change your behavior, it can trigger changes in others. So, weed first your own garden. Understand your anger triggers so you can quickly process new anger. Take deep breaths, count, sing, laugh, whistle, anything to get back your control.

Once, when her loving mom was droning on in advice groove, my daughter started to laugh. Her boyfriend turned and asked, "What the heck are you laughing at?"

"Sometimes you just have to laugh, because if you don't you'll cry." At that, we all laughed. The tension I created without intending to cleared.

A cup brimful of sweet water cannot spill even one drop of bitter water however suddenly jolted.—Amy Carmichael

Anger, Heat that Burns

Anger happens in direct response to our inability to control someone or something. The difficult people in your life think stupid things, blame you for things that are not your fault, do things you don't want them to do, and don't do what you want them to do when you want them to do it. You get angry because they have the nerve to behave that way. They get angry with you because they feel the same way about your behavior.

No matter how hard you work on yourself, you're bound to get angry. What makes you angry is good information for self-growth and development. Instead of worrying about getting back at what set

Anger, Heat that Burns Exercise

Look at your own reactions to anger and answer these questions:

What do you do when someone yells or acts angry with you?

Does your reaction depend on who is angry?

Write your answers in the context of the action you take and the differences depending on their relationship with you. Are you inclined to get angry back or walk away? Do you seek out someone to talk with about it? Do you purposely avoid coming in contact with people you know have tempers?

Next look at what makes you angry and answer these questions:

Think back through your childhood to three times you can remember feeling really angry.

Think back over the last year to three times you can remember feeling really angry.

This time, for each angry incident, answer each of these four questions:

you off, seek to discover why it raised your dander. Take deep breaths, count to a hundred if you have to, anything to keep yourself from reacting. Make responding rationally your goal. Refuse to let anger immobilize you.

Here's my formula for dissolving my anger. For fury, I pull out the heavy artillery of deep breaths, prayer, and meditation. Most times, I dive into the eye of my storm. Learn what emotions are driving the wind. Among the choices are fear of something, approval issues, security issues, or control issues. Understanding calms the storm enough for me to decide what I want and how to get it. Sometimes I'll talk the problem over with someone to come up with my options. Then, immediately I take the necessary action, so I can then let go of the outcome. I give the problem my best shot. That frees me up intellectually and emotionally so I can go about my business.

Anger stimulus requires response, intellectually and emotionally, and we ignore the emotional part at our peril. You fool yourself if you expect anger to disappear like the sun at night. Recognize that suppressing anger is an action, and anger becomes a terrible inner beast when suppressed. When anger comes up for you, the generic choices are to let it out, hold it in, or work it off. The healthy response comes from working anger off by solving the problem or using up the angry energy.

The action part of my guidelines usually involves some kind of constructive confrontation. Here's my formula for constructive confrontation:

1. Be ready with all facts, nothing but the facts, and make sure your facts are right. Check and double-check, because the tough ones will do their best to shoot holes in them.

2. Know all your important issues and focus only within the context of those issues. Never depend on your memory for this step. Write your game plan on paper. Confrontation is stressful. You could forget something important.

3. Put yourself in the other person's shoes and write out every possible option available to each of you.

4. With your written game plan, keep your focus, and keep yourself from getting trapped in ruts off your plow line. Keep your wits sharp so you know when the other person's pulling you off point and outside your focus area.

Sometimes the best decision means walking away and letting go of the loss. Some battles aren't worth your time or your stress.

1. *Who or what made you angry?*
2. *Why did that situation trigger such anger?*
3. *Would that same situation make you just as angry today?*
4. *Why or why not?*

Unhealthy anger responses become almost limitless. Letting anger out through displacement means someone gets angry at you about something you had nothing to do with—you get the anger because you are handy or easy. Projection lets people dump all kinds of nasty remarks your way, usually by lying or saying they come from sources other than themselves. The sneaky passive-aggressive have a bag of tricks too big for any book. After an argument, PA's can bring about their versions of *Gaslight* time at your house. All of a sudden you lose things, can't remember being told things, and find out that you aren't getting your mail or telephone messages. PA's can put you through a lot of frustration before you catch on, and you may never catch on. Sometimes, procrastination comes from a passive-aggressive response, as does depression, which emotionally removes the depressed from the relationship.

Anger is a stimulus which requires a response. When you deal with your anger when it comes up, analyze its cause, and do what works for you to return to a calm state, and you will be happier and healthier than most people. When you carry around your anger you are like a truck carrying fertilizer. Everybody knows what you're carrying.

Most important of all, you know what you are carrying. You lie to yourself, pretending to think and feel one way when you really think and feel another. That destroys your integrity and self-esteem. You become ashamed of yourself at some level and that can grow into self-pity. You become a pathetic mess and you've done it all to yourself. When you realize that, you can become clinically depressed.

Think of stuffed anger like emotional fat that grows inside you unless you choose to lose it. If you don't want to become emotionally obese, you need to work off each pound of anger you put on.

My mother, a stuffer, had a husband and daughter with little short fuses. She taught me at an early age: When you get angry tear paper into little pieces, punch a pillow, run around the block, ride your bicycle, or do some hard work, like scrubbing the floor. I remember one night when I was furious, I cleaned the whole apartment, even the oven. When I finished I was as relaxed and refreshed as if I had had a great night's sleep.

Many people fail to realize that anger is energy. Anger, based in fear, brings about the flight or fight syndrome. To stay mentally, spiritually and emotionally healthy, you have to find your own way of burning off that energy. And it is highly usable energy.

The first time my oldest daughter did not come home before midnight, anger raged in me, because I knew intellectually she was testing me. Yet, emotionally my heart fueled fear of the worst. I went downstairs to the recreation room, turned on aerobics music, and wrote an entire choreographed routine. By the time she came home around 3 a.m., I dealt with the situation rationally.

As a single parent, the responsibilities of raising the children alone weighed heavily on me. When the children would fight, it scared me. When I'm gone, they are all they have. One Sunday afternoon one had hurt the other in a fight. My rage was uncontainable. I said, *I'm tired of this fighting between you two and I'm leaving.* I took my rage outside into Valley Forge Park in Pennsylvania and walked off my anger for hours along the streams there, smelled the air, the trees, heard the birds, watched the water. When I came back home, my two daughters looked at me like two deer in headlights, and they never fought like that in front of me again. However, my downstairs neighbor, years later, told me that one day he thought they were going to kill each other over a pencil.

Obviously you can't throw your anger at others every time it comes up. You need to act out of the personal choices open to you. You can't force people to change the behaviors that annoy you, however, you can make choices that make their annoying behavior less desirable for them. Another example. Your spouse, with remote in hand, has sex with you while still keeping track of the various sports on television. You get furious, feel used. You say, *Come on, turn off the television.* Grudgingly, he pushes the power button on the remote. He did what you wanted, but the sex has still been spoiled for both of you.

Understand that saying nothing gives only a grudged peace. If you fail to say something really annoys you, not only are you unlikely to forget it, but also they're going to keep on doing it. Why? Because your silence teaches them that it is okay to treat you that way. So, you are likely to find yourself in the same position again and holding anger in between. It would be better to analyze why having the television on annoys you when you make love. Yes, it would annoy most people, yet the reasons for their anger are individual. Possibilities—feel hurt, stupid, used, unloved, unimportant, inhuman, or move into a delighted elation in revenge mode. Yes, some people turn anger into revenge and really enjoy getting even.

In this situation someone has decided, without any discussion with you, that it works to make love while tracking the games. Like them, you can decide, without any discussion with them, that sharing attention with the television does not work when you make love. Here are personal behavior actions that ask nothing of the other person:

You choose to disappear after a couple of kisses when the television is on. You say, only if asked, making love with the television on doesn't do it for me.

When you know that television sports are the entertainment for a block of time, you find something to do that is fun for you.

Each of these actions, and you can probably think of more, have you taking personal responsibility for your own happiness. You've taken away another person's power to ruin your happiness. And this behavior teaches people how to treat you in a positive way, the same way ignoring unacceptable behavior teaches people how to treat you in a negative way.

Life is conflict. No two people are exactly alike. Our differences lead to anger. Anger is a normal reaction when our world does not behave according to our assumptions, presumptions, perceptions, and expectations. Angry people feel out of control of their situation and get angry to get back in control.

Neither sex holds the patent on anger. Most carry some semblance of resentment or hidden anger inside. Yet women resist blowing up or hiding out and tend toward talking it out, while men tend toward blowing up or hiding out, anything but talking it out.

Still, normal, meaning psychologically unremarkable or mentally healthy, men and women cite similar reasons that provoke their anger:

- Dishonesty
- Violating privacy
- Unappreciated
- People who won't do their fair share
- Making unreasonable demands
- Feeling unloved in a committed relationship
- People who don't listen
- Rigid, judgmental, critical behavior
- Ridicule disguised as humor

These behaviors make people feel frustrated, threatened, defensive, needy, undervalued, and overpowered. None of these acts against us goes unnoticed. Some of us are able to speak up right away, but most of us can't think of the right words to say when it happens. Oh, we're terrific in the car on the way home or talking with someone later about it. At the time it happens, most of us tend to stuff it. So, the stuffers respond by ignoring, giving in, coping, compromising, delaying response, and some squeal to anyone who will listen. In comparison, the speakouts get defensive or retaliate either passively or aggressively, which can also mean squealing to anyone who will listen.

- Both the stuffers and the speakouts operate in relationship vacuums which leave at least one person the loser:
- Ignore the Problem or Avoidance is I lose, you lose.
- Giving in or Accommodating is You win, I lose.
- Active or Passive Aggression is I hurt, you suffer.
- Compromise is You lose, I lose.

Neither the stuffers nor the screamers have honest relationships. Neither is happy; however, the screamers are probably healthier. According to University of Michigan research scientist, Mara Julius, Ph.D., people who suppressed anger and had high blood pressure had a five times greater risk of dying when compared to people who did not suppress anger.

Connections have also been made between suppressed anger and psoriasis and other skin diseases, heart disease, cancer, and rheumatoid arthritis.

For example, a quiet family man with a screamer wife habitually stuffed his anger to keep the peace. When he was told one night his teenage daughter was pregnant, he died of a massive heart attack within two hours, even though he was healthy with no personal history or family history of heart disease.

Healthy disagreement, anger, frustration demand dialogue. The optimum conflict resolution strategy is Win-Win, where disagreements are resolved with cooperation and collaboration. Before that can happen, each person involved in a conflict needs to understand the other's position.

Aristotle said that anyone can become angry—that is easy. But to be angry with the right person, to the right degree, at the right time, for the right purpose, and in the right way—this is not easy.

Three truths can help you tremendously in conflict situations:

1. Others have a right to their feelings and opinions.

2. You have a right to your feelings and opinions.

3. Each of you has choice.

Depending on your personality, each one of the three truths may be a difficult concept for you. The domineering devalue others' feelings and opinions, believing they know best. The dominated have suffered so much pain by speaking up, they may no longer consciously acknowledge their feelings or opinions.

You may be thinking: *Easy for you to say that I have this great choice. When I speak up, lover goes into cave, and I get no conversation, no company, no help, and no sex.* That's the way it goes in many relationships, because people don't exercise their own freedom to choose their response in any given situation. Or they fail to realize they make a personal choice to give in so the other person won't go in the cave. They exercise their free choice because of their belief that person is the only person on the planet they want to have conversation with, keep company with, get help from. The sex part becomes a moral issue, however, which can violate commitments and marriage vows. As long as people give in under threat of cave, the other person will use it as leverage to dominate them.

Cave copers outnumber screamers by about 9:1. Cave copers become lost to you once they enter the cave. Like a child who has tantrums, they need to understand that that behavior is unacceptable in the relationship. I know, *easy for you to say.* Recognize cave copers will use that strategy as long as it works for them. When you stop automatically giving in, cave essentially stops working. That doesn't mean the cave coper will come right out and say, "You win, you can have your way." It does stop being an automatic win and opens a window for you to begin a dialogue.

Pick a time when your agendas are clear and both of you are up to dialogue about relationship problems. For example, at a time when you two are enjoying each other's company, you can ask for a block of time to discuss some feelings you are having about your relationship. Again, I know, *easy for you to say when the time they'll say is the tenth of doomsday.* Persist and make it happen. How much of a relationship do you have anyway when your partner refuses to speak with you about something in your relationship that has you hurting?

Recognize, however, that changing your behavior abruptly could end the relationship. If you are in a relationship where you have taught someone that cave threats stop your argument, that person is not going to like it when cave threats don't work with you any more.

Your partner obviously has choice to find someone else who gives in when cave is threatened.

Truth be told, fear of the relationship ending makes people put up with all kinds of dominating behavior from other people. Again, that is choice. I'm counting on you to want good relationships since you are reading this book. I'm also counting on you to do the hard stuff that enables you to get them and keep them.

When someone is actively acting out angry emotions with you, the only relief for them is creating a better situation. That being said, what do you do when someone is venting in your face? Adapt the rule of the hole—When you are in one, don't dig. So, when someone is angry with you, avoid making them angrier. Disagreeing with them, of course, makes them angrier. They are angry and want to fight and you fall into their hole when you fight back. Conversely, finding agreement helps diffuse the anger. Would it be so hard to merely acknowledge the person's anger by saying, *I can understand how that would make you angry*. No constructive problem-solving happens while anyone is actively acting-out in anger. So the basics are: acknowledge anger, let the person vent, and when the anger is diffused allow some space before you move into problem-solving. The basics for resolving relationship conflicts seem simple to understand and extremely hard to do without a committed mission statement.

Here's the Relationship Conflict Resolution Mission Statement: I commit myself to do whatever it takes to understand how you feel, why you feel that way, and what you want, and I ask you to commit to understanding how I feel, why I feel that way, and what I want. Put it in writing.

Here's the mission stated in fair fighting rules:

1. Both of you have to decide who goes first.
2. Each of you has to listen actively, holding judgment and criticism, with only the goal to understand the other well enough to repeat your understanding to the satisfaction of the other.

3. Both of you have to commit to collaboration and cooperation to find fair resolution of the issue.

Here are the communication skills to help you resolve conflict, using the fair fighting rules:

1. Self Analysis—Know first why this particular issue pushes your buttons so easily. Is the issue for you about fear, approval, control, or security?
2. Mutually Agree on a Time for Discussion—To avoid a tenth of doomsday response, give a time frame, like "This week I would like you to make some time to discuss . . . "
3. Acknowledge Anger, Frustration, Fear—Suspend your disbelief and accept the reality of the other person's feelings at the moment and withhold any judgment or criticism. No one's feelings seem stupid, silly or ridiculous to them at times when anger and emotions rule them.
4. Seek First Common Ground—Instead of making what you disagree with your target, make what you agree with your target. How you do that is to agree with any truth, probability of truth, and general truth allowing you to agree in principle.
5. Allow the Person to Vent—Patiently listen without interrupting, using body language and short phrases, such as I see . . . Oh, I didn't realize that . . . I can see that is important to you, to let the people know you are really hearing them.
6. Avoid Accusing, Assuming, and Keep Them Focused on the Specific Situation—Your only hope of hearing the real reason for the anger comes from listening actively and saving your issues for your turn.
7. Find Out What the Person Wants and What They Are Willing to Do to Get it—After you've listened to what they don't want, it's important to find out what they do want. You need to get and give that information to move on to collaboration and cooperation.

8. Resolve to Keep Control of Your Emotions—Remember your goal is to understand from the other person's point of view so you can repeat it to move on to your turn.
9. Allow the Angry Person to Save Face—Find a way to honor their feelings, opinions, and right to free choice without compromising your own. For example, you can agree to disagree.

Here are some behaviors that prevent and reduce anger: fair, flexible, open-minded, respectful soft voice, sharing honest and blame-free feelings, and laser-beam focus on practical solutions.

Anger happens in relationships, even when people love each other, maybe especially because people love each other. Own the problems anger causes. Understand anger dynamics. Then and only then can you decide whether to choose to act upon the anger directly, react to it indirectly, or release it. The more skillfully you analyze the dynamics that led up to an angry situation, the more likely you are to release your angry energy and let it go. And that's not wimping out. That is choosing your battles. You just can't fight them all. You're never going to make your world perfect for you and if you try, you'll spend most of your life in heat without having the fun of hot times.

Here are some guidelines to help you diffuse out-of-control conflict situations, so you can avoid getting sucked into a scream-fest, and keep your head when someone screams and yells at you:

1. Match the tone of voice without the anger.
2. Give the person your full attention with eye contact.
3. Move to the side of a person, since face-to-face equals conflict posture.
4. Make yourself appear as small as possible, arms together, head lowered, one hip out.
5. Determine to define the problem by listening, asking for specifics, and exploring all sides of the issue.

6. Acknowledge the angry feelings with understanding without necessarily agreeing with them.
7. Catch them off-guard with humor: *Wait one second—let me call the Pope and ask him to call all his bishops into prayer for clean shirts for you!*

This diffuser works with children's tantrums and teaches them they can make choices to control their anger. *Right now I would like to blow up a big balloon and stuff it into your mouth, but I am not going to do that because you wouldn't be able to breathe and you could die. So, I am choosing not to put a balloon into your mouth. I can't always do what I want to do and neither can you. What we can usually do is try to work out something that can work for both of us. Would you like to try and do that?*

Many people ask me in workshops: *How do I know when the anger no longer falls inside the lines of normal frustration?* That's a good question, and most people in abusive relationships usually know the answer when they ask the question. One or more of these situations red flag out-of-control anger:

- Uses anger to domineer and control others.
- Anger frequent, intense, and episodes last too long.
- Sometimes leads to physical aggression.
- Anger irrational.
- People are afraid, anxious when this person's around.
- Uses anger tantrums to get their way.
- Others become afraid to do anything without asking permission.
- Person says ridiculing, criticizing, insulting is only kidding.
- Angry person minimizes, denies, and blames abuse on victim.

Abusive people often apologize after one of their out-of-control episodes and expect instant forgiveness. Be realistic about apologies. Apologies may stop the flow of blood, literally or figuratively, but they don't heal the sore spot. An apology is like digging a hole and leaving it. Without having planted a seed of forgiveness, feeding it and watering it, no one deserves harvesting forgiveness they haven't taken positive action to get.

True remorse and contrition manifest in earning forgiveness to overcome the instability their behavior created. Admitting wrong and asking for forgiveness without actually making some kind of reparation of good against the bad done simply adds to the bad done. That puts all the responsibility on the injured party and in effect adds insult to injury, while the one who has done wrong has enjoyed the wrong and then expects to enjoy forgiveness without making retribution.

Thoughtless, selfish behavior hurts people emotionally and spiritually. The person who does the hurting needs to accept responsibility for healing the hurt they caused. Try this when people important to you do something for which they say they are sorry. Ask them: *How are you going to pay your sorry?* This places a responsibility to heal the hurts they cause. Recognizing that their hurtful behavior will be expected to be healed in some way just may discourage repeating previous hurtful behavior that they got away with a simple *I'm sorry*. Of course, that also means that they are likely to expect you to do the same. This helping the injured party heal approach in relationships makes each party accountable for the damage and pain caused by thoughtless, selfish and self-centered behavior.

Active and Passive Getting Even – The Four Faces of Revenge

Basically, we get angry at real and imaginary wrongs against us. Being wronged doesn't feel good, so, within the context of stimulus and response, we must do something to feel better. Our choices range from healthy to unhealthy:

- ❖ Release the anger and let it go.
- ❖ Process the anger to determine cause.
- ❖ Choose to respond to the anger instead of react.
- ❖ Repress the anger, essentially swallowing it.
- ❖ Harbor feelings of ill will.
- ❖ Take an unfriendly, spiteful action.
- ❖ Add the bitterness of hate.
- ❖ Engage in mean-spirited action.
- ❖ Grow the anger to full fury and inflict destructive wrath, a cold, ruthless revenge that shows neither mercy nor pity, and cannot forgive.

Good emotional management asks us to think through a response to our anger instead of automatically reacting. Neutral becomes the default goal of emotional management, so anger, fear, and expectations can't negatively color our present moment situational responses. Within the context of good emotional management, positive anger management cautions us to watch out for wrong, unhealthy attempts at revenge.

Anger, by itself, a pure emotion, exists. Angry emotions come up for us time and again all our lives. Healthy response focuses on situations and acts directly. Unhealthy response focuses on people to lay blame and make them pay for what they did.

In the more extreme instances of out-of-control anger, another emotion, hatred, contaminates our thinking, figuratively poisoning our minds. Unlike angry emotions that flare up, cool down, and go away, hatred takes root with the survival determination of a maple sapling. In my yard, the little buggers grow up between little cracks in two-inch bricks.

Retaliation, choosing to get even, wears two faces. The so-called just face of righteous anger against those who deserve punishment for their wrongs, and revenge, the unjust desire to spitefully and maliciously pay someone back for wrongs arise out of feelings of bitterness and hatred.

Revenge is a choice when uncontrolled stimuli of anger, ire, rage, and fury demand a response. Ideally, that response aims to eliminate the dissatisfaction from the situation that provoked the anger. The unhealthy response lusts after retaliation, to exact payment for the trouble suffered, the scenario commonly labeled *revenge*. You did this and I am one down. I did that, and we are again even.

Hot anger, during processing, can cool into cold, calculating revenge. Anger, at its highest escalation—fury—acts to destroy when loss of emotional control increases toward madness. This reaction lawyers term *temporary insanity* in pleas to judges and juries for mercy for their clients, thereby asking for something their clients failed to feel for their victims.

Revenge sprouts a variety of bitter fruit and makes the subject of whole books. Here we look at four faces of revenge: VIOLENCE, PASSIVE AGGRESSION, PROCRASTINATION, and DEPRESSION. Violence, active aggression, suddenly attempts to or actually hurts and/or destroys. Passive aggression, like slow poison, attempts revenge without engaging in conflict, often under cover. Procrastination, going limp, when we cannot, will not, or do not choose to act, sometimes works against others, like a slow-down or work-stoppage strike. Finally, depression, a shut-down paralysis of going fallow, like procrastination, can act against another by removing our active selves from access to them. The depressed essentially stop being mentally and emotionally home.

You've heard the sounds and fury of revenge. *I don't get mad, I get even. I did what I did out of pure, delicious spite. They deserved it. I wish you could have seen their faces at pay-back time. No matter how long it takes, I'll be sure to even this score. I keep my enemies close and clueless, keeping tabs on what they are up to, so I can get even when they least expect it. I'll show them. Nobody messes with me without suffering for it. If I can't have you, nobody will. I'll make your life hell if you go ahead with that plan.*

Violence, Quick Destruction

Violence, a punitive act of power over the weak, attacks the dignity of a person. Everyone is vulnerable, since no one can prevent or predict random acts of violence. They occur in the workplace, relationships, homes, on the street, in vehicles from drive-by shootings, out of arguments, in hospitals, restaurants, post offices, on airplanes, and anywhere people go.

Out-of-control people persecute those in their lives and in their environment with their addictions, whether anger, alcohol, drugs, or sex. Self-destructive, these individuals have no right to make anyone suffer for the problems they create by their choices and lifestyles. Yet the suffering they heap on others is incalculable.

Living in abusive relationships devastates and breaks people's spirits, because the abuse comes from those who are supposed to love them. The abuser and the abused represent two extremes of loss of power: anger and sadness. Both give up power over self.

The human dignity of the abused soon becomes unable to withstand the onslaught against it, and withers, sometimes disappearing altogether. Without dignity to give them strength of purpose, victims in unhealthy relationships fail to comprehend how to save themselves before their situation destroys them, physically or emotionally. Children are the most helpless abuse victims.

So many times when abusive situations come out of the closet, friends and family wonder, How did such a nice person end up with such a horrible person? The terrible reality—the abuser planned it that way. Controlling personalities nearly always choose for their partners the most agreeable, people pleasing, least assertive, undemanding individuals. They find strong, assertive individuals with high self-esteem far too much trouble to control.

These nice victims often give abusers a free ride for a long time. The newly abused don't talk about their relationship problems because they are embarrassed or they think their problems are trivial or explainable. In the beginning, most of the abuse is verbal. The abused frequently enable the abusers, shielding them with excuses for their strange behavior: *It's not so bad. Everybody gets mad once in a while. You have to expect some bad times in relationships. I'll just be more careful from now on so Lover Who Must Be Obeyed doesn't get so upset. I'm not perfect, either.*

As time goes on, the abuse worsens, episodes get closer together, and abuse becomes a way of life for victims. They acclimate themselves to their life of abuse, in the same kind of numbing vacuum as the frog in a hot water experiment. The experimenter wanted to know how hot the water would have to be before the frog would jump out of the beaker. But the frog never jumped and boiled to its death. A cruel experiment. Yet it explains how the abused lull themselves into a false reality where they no longer are connected close enough to reality to react appropriately to danger. The frog in the experiment would have instantly jumped from hot water, but when the water heated slowly, it did not. Likewise, most abuse victims would have left if the abuse began with hours of critical tirades or blood and broken bones.

The adage, *We learn what we live* can acclimate a victim to secret abuse for a long time. Certain social scientists believe the more exposure we have to yelling, criticism, bad language, and violence, the greater our tolerance for them. Tolerance also means resorting to those behaviors. That's why so many of the abused become abusers. In abuse situations, victims' emotions run the gamut from stress to full-blown anxiety. Spurts of anger get them nowhere or make matters worse. Depression is common. Surrounded by guilt, self-blame, and numbed by depression, they begin a cycle of emotional drought, living mechanical days.

Relatives and friends often ask the victim: *Why didn't you tell me? Why didn't you go for help? Why didn't you leave long ago?*

Why have you allowed this to go on for so long? The victims, with dignity and self-worth near empty, have no logical answers. These critical, blaming questions heap more hurt on victims who have no logical answers. Few have enough dignity and self-esteem left to counter back, *Why aren't you asking why my abuser did this to me?*

The common reasons victims give:

- ❖ I didn't tell you because I love my partner, and I kept hoping it would get better.
- ❖ I didn't go for help because I didn't have the money, either because of our finances or because my partner controls the money and I couldn't get at it.
- ❖ I didn't leave because I had no where to go and I was too embarrassed to ask somebody to take me in.
- ❖ Except for my partner's outbursts, we have a nice place to live, good income, and basically a good life.
- ❖ I didn't want this relationship to fail, too.

The reasons most abused victims rarely tell anyone:

- ❖ I felt so ashamed and pitiful I didn't want anyone to know.
- ❖ I felt I'd put my children, my family, and my co-workers in danger.
- ❖ I was afraid of being alone; if I left, I wouldn't have anyone.
- ❖ I felt worthless, like I would be nothing without my partner.

The victims' plight becomes so familiar, so normal they actually resist change within the context of *The devil I know is better than a devil I don't know.* Of course it makes no sense. Yet, neither does an abusive relationship.

The abused often hone expert skills, however, at strategizing, concealing their troubles, making creative excuses for their abusive partners, explaining away bruises, lying to medical professionals, and pretending their lives are working.

Refusal to get help confounds family and friends of victims. Many victims experience little of the abusive behavior before they make their commitment. The first time it happens, they go through the trauma of shock, disbelief, frustration, and anger. They wonder, *Why is this happening to me?*

In unhealthy relationships, speaking to friends, family, and professionals marshals needed support. I believe that people in unhealthy relationships can only solve their problems with support and professional intervention. When an abuse victim tells a friend about her relationship problems, the friend can serve as a reality check. *That's not normal behavior. That person needs help. I am afraid for you. You are in danger there. You have let this situation go on too long and you are living in an abusive relationship.* Sharing problems lets the victims know the perpetrators, not they, are responsible for the abuse.

Like the frog in the experiment, most unhealthy physical relationships begin in a comfortable environment. Out of nowhere comes that first slap and an *I'm sorry.* A weak character accepts the apology, while a strong character leaves and never looks back. A strong character with high self-esteem seems to know right away that physical anger comes from unhealthy people who can't or won't control their emotions. They live by my mother's adage, *If it happens once, shame on you. If it happens twice, shame on me.* Does that mean you can never have a healthy relationship once someone has gotten physical? Unlikely and possible. Bullies bully those they can bully. However, if the average person wants to stay in a relationship after one party has gotten physical, something has to change within the person who got physical so that it never happens again. That change can be a commitment to self-control or professional intervention with recognition that there will never be a second physical outburst in your relationship. Could there be an odd situation where a happy couple fist-fights regularly? Certainly. However, that situation is not violence, since neither partner fits the hurt victim profile or the power-hungry abuser profile. Neither partner claims and exercises power over the other as what happens in abusive situations.

Most times, getting away with that first slap usually leads the abuser to inflict more physical abuse. Slaps escalate, sometimes with long periods in between, to pushes, hits, black-and-blue marks, punches, then lost teeth and broken bones.

Unhealthy emotional relationships usually begin a bit differently. At first you are the most wonderful person on the planet and your wish is the other person's command. After you make your commitment, however, the fault-finding begins. At first, little picky things, then the criticisms get more and more damning, the changes you are asked to make get more difficult, with the control getting tighter and tighter.

Here's my story. Young and naive, I married a handicapped man with low self-esteem, believing my love could make up for everything and make him happy. You can see from that reasoning I set myself up for big trouble from the get-go. Our daughter was an infant the first time he slapped my face. Shocked, I ran across the second-level porch to my neighbor. He said, "You mean you left your baby in there with him?" He made me feel like a bad mother. I felt guilty and ran back in. I found no help outside, only condemnation. The second time he slapped my face my children were two and four, and, this time, my lip was bleeding. The next violent incident came when my children were five and seven. My husband tried to corner me in the kitchen. I picked up one of those big iron skillets and told him if he came any closer, I'd hit him with it. He laughed, said "Ha!," came closer, and got hit.

Twice past the "shame on me" time, I still didn't leave. That same year, I had fibroid tumors that required a hysterectomy. There were problems with the surgery. The doctor came into my hospital room and told me if he couldn't solve the problem, I would die. My first thought as a staunch Catholic mother of two: If I live, I will not live the rest of my life with this man. I had a six-month recovery in front of me. My first day home, I told my husband I was leaving him as soon as I healed. He could stay or he could go. It wouldn't make any difference, but I would, of course, prefer he left. He wouldn't leave and played a model husband with a few lapses here and there.

One lapse could have been a fatal one. The night before the children and I were scheduled to move he had brought over two people to wear me down and change my mind about leaving. At about 9 p.m. when he realized it hadn't worked, he told me my decision didn't matter anyway because he had canceled the mover.

Shocked, I called the mover. Sure enough, he had canceled and the mover said he didn't want to get involved in domestic problems. Undaunted and determined, I took out the telephone book and called every mover with my story until one mover said he would do it. Then he said, "And you tell your husband if he gives us one iota of trouble we'll tie his legs in a bow and stuff his feet into his mouth."

Soon after I left, during the time he was stalking, breaking car windows, trying to get into my apartment, threatening to kill my parents, the children let him into the apartment. He had come to rape me. I told him to wait until the children were asleep. While I was getting undressed in the living room, I took a sting gun from the closet that looked like a German Luger and pointed it at him and told him to leave. He left. I called the police. We went to court. He was fined and I got a protective order. I never saw him again.

To this day, I feel ashamed of getting myself into such a relationship and rarely speak of it. I tell it here to provide a greater understanding of how hard it is for victims in abusive relationships to make the hard decision to give up and leave. Leaving admits the failure of a committed relationship entered into with love and good faith. It also says, *My love isn't good enough to make this person I love happy.* And that may be the hardest reality to accept. Those are the two reasons why I stayed as long as I did.

Be as supportive, understanding, empathetic, and nonjudgmental as you can when someone you know is struggling in an unhealthy relationship. Life on the abusive edge is awful.

One more important reality. When my husband tried cornering me in the kitchen, he wasn't yelling. He just had that look. Avoid a false sense of security, believing yelling comes before violence. Full-blown fury many times speaks with a soft, amazingly controlled voice. Whether you find yourself in a violent situation with someone you know or a stranger, protecting yourself requires skill, purpose, and laser focus on survival.

Know that violent personalities can, and usually do, contain both Jekyll and Hyde. Violent strangers lure their victims initially, not with guns, orders, or physical force, but with charm, offers of help, and appeal to a person's desire to behave kindly toward others. After the fact, many victims say they felt uneasy. Something told them to get away from this person, that something seemed wrong, but they ignored their internal red flags.

Perhaps the best tactic for avoiding violent encounters with strangers may be listening to your sixth sense, intuition, or whatever you call it when your inner voice talks to you.

Not too long ago, while walking my dog, I noticed a good-looking man looking at me while he talked with some people. As soon as he saw me, he left them and came toward me with an excited look and a smiling face, like he knew me. I didn't know him, but felt a spark of attraction.

I bet I can surprise you by telling you what nationality you are. I replied, "Oh!" Then he proceeded to tell me, along with other interesting things about me that he, as a stranger, had no business knowing. The whole time he spoke, he kept interrupting himself to say big hellos to people we passed. Before long he name-dropped prominent socialites, and pressed hard for me to have coffee or tea with him. By this time, my gut had moved into red-alert mode. "I'm sorry, I have the dog." Undaunted, he said, "Wait right here. I'll make it all right with them." He went into the coffee bar. Stupidly frozen, I waited, overwhelmed by the whole situation, instead of disappearing. Still, without the powerful onslaught of charm, I had space to think.

Surprising someone on the street stating personal information about them seemed neither normal nor respectful. Name-dropping usually means to impress. He didn't dress like someone who hobnobs with the rich and famous. And, he wore no coat on a cool, fall day. When he came out, he said, "They won't do it, but why don't we just sit outside?" I thanked him for his offer, told him I was chilly, and needed to get home. He kept right on talking and walking. My intuition told me not to annoy him. Might I also add the dog wanted no part of him. So I walked block after block, hoping he would get either cold or tired. He finally said he had to go.

When someone is up to no good, they blow out the details fast and furious. You feel like you're in the eye of a storm, and can get temporarily blindsided, like I did. That's on purpose. They don't want you to have time to think, process, compare, contrast, or discern.

Besides charm, violent perpetrators may try to goad you into talking with them. *You probably feel you're too good to talk with the likes of me.* Nothing you can say works to your benefit. Treat the comment as a degrading lure, silently walk away, or, if you can't, break eye contact and remain silent.

One other trick puts people seemingly into a perpetrator's debt. After a perpetrator offers help, many women find it hard to get rid of the helper.

When a stranger vies for your attention like you are the most wonderful person on the planet, keep your brain in gear. You need to discern if the attention is a budding friendship or a bum's rush.

Recognize that the victims of violence are not always males against women and children. Violence strikes young and old alike in situations of male against male, female against female, female against male, old against young, and children against others.

Passive Aggression, Slow Poison

The insidious nature of passive-aggressive (PA) behavior, with its subtle secrecy, mostly frees PA's from being suspected of wrongdoing. While they make life miserable for others, PA's outwardly appear easy-going, friendly, polite, cooperative, gentle, and nice.

Their refusal to engage in conflict doesn't, however, mean they give up getting their way. What PA's want remains uppermost in their minds and they just go get it. If it's important to them, what you want won't matter.

Anyone, and everyone at one time or another, engages in conflict-avoiding passive-aggressive behavior. Some people are passive-aggressive outside the home and aggressive in their homes. Within the home, some people are passive-aggressive with their spouses and aggressive with their children. Consider also the meek and mild people who become Atilla the Hun behind the wheels of their cars.

Here are some of the ways PA's get even with people who annoy them:

- ❖ Lateness and Procrastination
- ❖ Physically Hiding Another's Belongings
- ❖ Withdrawal, including Sexual Availability
- ❖ Refusing to Cooperate
- ❖ Sarcasm, including Backhanded Compliments
- ❖ Sarcasm, including Unfavorable Comparisons
- ❖ Gossip
- ❖ Secretly Disabling Another's Equipment
- ❖ Secretly Destroying or Damaging Another's Property

PA's often exaggerate the eye-for-an-eye concept by countering a small hurt with a bigger payback. *You keep complaining because I don't spend enough time with you.* Here are some ways PA's might pay back. *I won't even call you for two weeks. I'll take a second job. I'll come home late every night. I'll start a big personal project.*

Characteristic of PA's, they get their revenge just as much by not doing as by doing against, such as with procrastination. Some PA's habitually forget to tell you who called for you or visited you.

At work, pulling information out of a jealous PA co-worker can feel like pulling up a rosebush with bare hands. You can also count on a PA employee to call in sick the day a project is due or when they are expected to look after the office.

PA assistants are also expert at doing things exactly the way they know you would not want them done. Here's what one of my assistants did. I had cultivated the financial vice president of a large New York bank for weeks. While I was out of town I instructed my assistant to send out some letters I had previously dictated. She mixed up the bodies of the letters and the recipients. My big bank prospect got a letter intended for a wholesale florist. *I don't know what happened. I tried to get them out for you, just like you wanted. I was really busy. I am really sorry. I'll be glad to call them and tell them I'm sorry about the mistake*. Months later, I overheard the reason for her sabotage. *I don't know what's so special about her that they pay her such big bucks.*

PA's probably do their finest work with partners. While making dinner, I asked my boyfriend to please put away some boxes of herb tea into a large container. What he knew that I didn't know, that the teabags had no identifying tags, made the task he found initially annoying amazingly pleasurable. When I confronted him about what he had done, he said, "You sound annoyed with me. I can't believe you'd blame me for the problem when I just did what you told me to do." My jar of mystery tea delighted my surprise-loving friends for five years, as did the story of my long-gone PA boyfriend.

PA's often learn their craft early. This trick became fodder for the office humor mill every time somebody mentioned chicken and dinner in the same sentence. One time when a friend expected company for dinner, she asked her daughter to put the roasting chicken she had gotten ready the night before in the oven about a half hour before she was due home. The little dear put the chicken in the oven all right, plastic bag and all. Few things look more disgusting than an unbrowned chicken covered with melting plastic. Her daughter said, *But Mom, you didn't tell me to take the chicken out of the bag. You are so unfair. I can't believe you're blaming me when you're the one who forgot to tell me about the bag.*

For my older brother, teasing me became a favorite indoor sport. One afternoon, out of frustration, I snuck into his room while he did his paper route and poured glue over his wind-up 1950 Blue Ford Model. When he came home, he came downstairs with the car in his hand. *Barbara, I'm really sorry about this. Wow, I planned to surprise you and give you this car I know you always liked so much. But, now it's ruined. What a shame for you!*

Passive-aggressive behavior has its roots in immaturity, the underdeveloped personality not yet independent. Because PA's depend on others for approval, security, or to satisfy their need for control, they avoid active conflict and resort to sneaky, secret paybacks for real or imagined hurts or unsatisfied wants.

Sometimes, as with accident-prone PA's, their passive-aggressive acting out of hidden anger and resentment can be unconscious.

Much, if not all, passive-aggression is fear-based out of three needs: approval, security, and control. And each need manifests differently, although there can be overlap.

1. The Passive-Aggressive Approval Seeker—A dependent type, this person needs support, approval, and reassurance. When they don't get their needs fulfilled, response comes mostly from the unconscious, because they are generally clueless that approval needs motivate their action.
2. The Passive-Aggressive Security Seeker—A defensive type, they worry and can become paralyzed into procrastination patterns. They fear doing the wrong thing, so they avoid change, and can stubbornly avoid even risking a new restaurant. At times inefficient, sullen, this personality rarely feels carefree and has a hard time letting loose and having fun. Out-of-control, these people can slowly adapt obsessive-compulsive behavior, like washing their hands dozens of times a day for fear of getting sick from other people's germs.

3. The Passive-Aggressive Controller—They hate conflict, don't like to argue at all, but covertly feel entitled to their own way. Their irritation with life and people can become hostility. They feel they deserve special attention and assume charge in situations where no one gave them permission to lead. Most times they throw temper tantrums or withdraw. Yet, like active aggressors, they can snap and get so frustrated, they become physical.

If strange things begin happening frequently at home or at the office, diary them as bad luck or possibly the work of a PA. Take special care to note where you put important items and papers. Count your money. Note times when people tell you they called or visited and you were not told. Only facts can break down the sophisticated denial mechanisms of the nice PA.

Watch out also for passive-aggression disguised as human foibles. Live-ins or visiting friends forget to tell you important things time after time. *I'm just so darn forgetful. I am so sorry. It's just the way I am, not really anything I can change.*

Proact against this type of PA excuse. Ask them to let the machine answer when you are not home. If they must answer, tell them to ask people to try you again since they forget to give you your messages. Remember your inaction against PA behavior that you know goes on becomes consent. Why give people permission to treat you thoughtlessly?

Passive-aggressive acts result from the buildup of unmanaged anger. Unmanaged anger, unprocessed, remains. It comes up, gets stuffed down, and stays.

Just because someone says nothing doesn't mean they plan to do nothing. PA's plan their attacks, both consciously and unconsciously, against themselves as well as others. Conscious PA acts can be underhanded and under cover or overt. Unconscious PA's get so preoccupied with their anger at another person or thing that they become ripe for accidents and mishaps.

An example of unconscious PA behavior. She wants him to go with her to the store. He refuses. Resentful, she goes alone. After checkout, she can't find her car keys. She roots through her purse and they are not where she keeps them. When she bends over to look on the floor by the counter, they fall out of her pocket. In the parking lot a heavy bag slips out of her hand on top of another bag and breaks a half-gallon bottle of orange juice. Instead of taking the leaking bottle out of the car, she closes the door and lets it run all over the seat. More frustrated and resentful than ever, and more preoccupied, she fails to see the parking lot pole and backs into it, jerking her neck. When she goes home, she tells her husband all that happened. He soothes her, rubs her neck, puts some cream on it, and tells her he'll make dinner as soon as he unloads the groceries and cleans up the car.

Does it cross his mind that it would have been easier if he had gone with her to the store? Is it likely he'll go the next time she asks? Does she realize her unmanaged anger distracted her mentally and physically and became the underlying force behind her orange juice and pole accidents?

PA's pay either too little attention to their feelings or they wallow in them, but rarely process them and let them go.

Here is an anger processing technique I call Options and Letting Go of Outcomes. Here's how it works. When something doesn't go your way, first look at your options. Here were some of hers:

Make an Appeal: "Look, I hate going to the store alone—won't you please come with me."

Take a Stand: "You never want to go to the store with me, even though you eat half the food. Like you, I have free choice. I choose never to go do the weekly shopping by myself."

Make a Demand: "I went to the store by myself last week. So it's your turn to go this week."

Negotiate: "Come on. If you go to the store with me, I'll go to the car races with you on Saturday."

After you choose and act on your option of choice, you let go of the outcome. Her evening no longer depends on what he does.

The personal problems of PA's punish others. They can't or won't deal directly with their problems and deny their PA behavior is premeditated. Let a PA know you are on to their dirty games and their PA acts can become more devastating and harder to pin on them.

Still, awareness and fact-finding are your only hope against a PA acting out against you. Pay attention, ask specific questions, gather facts, get agreements in writing, and use witnesses for support.

Can you fight PA behavior cool-headed every time? Sometimes your emotions will get in the way. Sometimes you won't even recognize it. Yet, every time you Option and Let Go of the Outcome, you're better off. In the shopping disaster, what if the heavy bag dropped on her foot and broke her toe? What if the car's frame bent on impact? Distraction can cause problems that extract from you needless suffering, time, and expense.

Unmanaged anger slithers out like a snake, striking and poisoning the lives of both the aggressors and their victims.

Turn the Option and Let Go of the Outcome process into a good habit to keep yourself free of stored anger and resentments. They do nothing good for you and can lead to distraction, disease, memory lapses, accidents, and other miseries.

Procrastination, Going Limp

Procrastination keeps increasing in popularity because it seems to work, a bad habit with great benefits. You can procrastinate to avoid doing what someone else wants you to do, avoid doing something you don't like doing, buy yourself time, and get even with those who annoy you.

Getting away with procrastination can be easy. When you decide to put something off, you know four things are likely to happen:

1. You can forget about it.
2. You may never have to do it.
3. Somebody else may do it.
4. You may get into trouble.

Three out of the four outcomes work for you. Sure, when you get into trouble, you feel uncomfortable. Clearly, though, the better odds fall on the side of procrastination and give the behavior enough support to hold its popularity.

Think of the great emotional benefits in releasing your mind to do the things you want to do. Procrastinators even have National Procrastinators' Week, a special week in March, to celebrate. Proud procrastinators may be so bold as to join the Procrastinators' Club of America, founded in 1956, and claiming thousands of members. Chronic procrastinators rationalize their behavior, citing their good intentions, and using their inability to change as their excuse.

Everyone puts things off, says *It's on my list.* Most people tolerate harmless omissions occasionally. Chronic procrastinators count on the patience of the people in their lives. Only when avoidance behavior becomes the rule rather than the exception, do people take notice. When people catch on that you are using procrastination to get out of doing your fair share, they balk.

At some point, many procrastinators come to the inevitable conclusion that putting things off leaves them on hold, erodes their self-confidence, and disappoints others. It creates internal conflict. Eventually you begin to feel lazy, irresponsible, and undisciplined. Broken promises haunt you. Harsh realities set in, like *Life doesn't wait until you have time for it.*

You know when you are not holding up your end, yet internal resistance keeps you from doing anything about it. Fear easily paralyzes chronic procrastinators who often lack discipline and may be commitment-phobic. Unsure of the way or the success of the outcome, procrastinators can get stuck in indecision. Projects loom before them like big red barns.

People who want to take responsibility, yet procrastinate, suffer from constant conflict. Their unfinished tasks plague them. They can't relax and enjoy themselves because of all the rotting crops in their fields. Deep inside they recognize *those who can, do, and those who can't, procrastinate.*

They'd like to get to the bottom of what's really going on, because they see themselves losing control. They know they aren't disorganized or lazy. Procrastinators often are subconsciously pained and that pain produces fear that paralyzes their ability to act. While they avoid doing, they also avoid facing feelings of inadequacy and protect their self-esteem. They can't fail at something they haven't done.

Here are common signs that put you at risk of procrastination paralysis:

- ❖ Perfectionist
- ❖ Energetic beginnings and abrupt standstill
- ❖ Amazing commitment; begins and finishes projects at the last minute
- ❖ Looks busy, but the activity doesn't produce recognizable results
- ❖ Takes a long time arriving at decisions and conclusions
- ❖ Puts out fires instead of preventing them
- ❖ Holds on to projects, refuses to delegate
- ❖ Neat freak who can't work if anything is disorganized
- ❖ Refuses help and doesn't want to discuss problems

Most procrastinators eventually feel the ripping sting of the downside: failed relationships, financial loss, job loss, and loss of opportunities. Once procrastinators begin to crash and burn, they become grim reapers indeed.

What many procrastinators can't often answer is why they aren't doing what they know needs to be done. Asking them why work is left to the last minute or fifteen minutes after never is like asking them to feed the chickens when they don't know what chickens look like. Before they can solve attacks of procrastination paralysis, they may need help to understand the underlying psychological reasons they consistently put things off.

The psychological roots of procrastination are buried and strong. You need to be alert to your psychological procrastination traps in particular situations in order to develop a system to rein in your procrastination. Any one or a combination of these procrastination profiles can sabotage even the best planning and scheduling system, resulting in procrastination on important tasks:

Deadline Superhero—Admit your addiction to the adrenaline rush of deadline thrills, your love of the challenge to finish against all odds. You bask as Superhero victorious at the edge of disaster. A beautiful thing, that feeling, a habit that pains you to think of breaking it.

The Procrastination Doctor's Prescription: Instead of one final deadline, force yourself to set several deadlines for projects and meet them one at a time. Prepare and pace yourself by meeting your step-by-step deadlines. Own the stress and arrogance of deadline thrills, the real possibility of disaster, and how the end product suffers from the lack of options in last-minute crunches. Face this horrible thought, proud Superhero: You may never know your best work.

Perfectionist—Catch yourself wanting everything perfect in an imperfect world. Look for feelings of insecurity, fear of making mistakes, and criticism. Like the Deadline Superhero, Perfectionists create built-in excuses for not doing their best work. *You have no right to criticize me when you won't give me enough time to do the job to the best of my ability.*

The Procrastination Doctor's Prescription: Work on understanding how you prioritize and label the importance of tasks and projects. Ask yourself why you bury yourself in details and spend so much time on the unimportant. Ask yourself what stops you from delegating tasks others could do so you can do the tasks no one else can. Demand of yourself the discipline to set priorities and assign realistic weight to tasks. Your best effort a day late may have little value. Your best effort within an on-time framework, while not quite as perfect, produces appropriate value.

Failure Flop Sweater—Nail yourself as afraid of failure, the likely reason you shrink from certain tasks.

The Procrastination Doctor's Prescription: Analyze the fear gaps one by one. Do you feel an ability gap? Do you believe you lack enough knowledge or experience to complete the task satisfactorily? Does something important to you hinge on the failure or success of this activity? Then bridge the gaps, plan the activity, and produce an acceptable result.

Success Flop Sweater—Nail yourself as afraid of greater and greater expectations as you move up the success ladder. You aren't quite sure you are up to the success of your efforts. Your self-esteem and self-confidence remain down some rungs. Most people fail to recognize this fear. One part of you wants to rocket up the ladder and another part fears falling on your face when you get there. That's why you seek challenges, begin enthusiastically, then begin a pattern of one postponement after another. In the back of your mind lurks the fear, *What happens if they ask me to do it again and I can't?*

The Procrastination Doctor's Prescription: Think through all parts of the task or project from beginning to end. When you know the number of rows in a field, you are less likely to stop plowing prematurely.

The Rebel—Own your joy in tweaking authority and the feelings of hostility and anger causing you to behave outside of what you know is expected of you. Does fear of control cause you to break the rules, your promises? Do you usually find yourself questioning another's intelligence or right to tell you to do something a certain way. Is it much easier to get you to do something if someone asks you rather than tells you?

The Procrastination Doctor's Prescription: It's easy to say *Accept your responsibilities appropriately and avoid stupid, stubborn refusal to maintain your need for control. It really annoys people.* Still, it can be helpful to look at what situations and which people trigger resistance-to-control issues for you. Consider resisting control as a form of resisting authority. *In control* means in charge, and *in charge* connotes authority.

Pressure Avoider—Bugging you is a need to cover up your faults and avoid the difficult. When this happens, you question your ability and can't find the motivation to get at the task. You dread the difficult because of the pressure the task puts on your lesser abilities, such as mechanics or math. You feel temperamentally incompatible with the tasks you avoid. Frustration sets in and you just can't get yourself to begin.

The Procrastination Doctor's Prescription: New learning comes from competence in doing something you've never done before. Sometimes the solution for avoidance procrastinators is a simple attitude adjustment. Just because the directions for the entertainment center were impossible to follow doesn't mean you'll have trouble putting the bicycle together. Asking for help doesn't mean you are stupid. Sometimes the most intelligent solution is asking for help from someone who has exceptional ability for the task. Other times, actually beginning the task solves most of the problem.

Big Thinkers/Dreamers—Expose your 'fraidy cat in denial. When the largeness of a task freeze-frames action, stop deluding yourself into believing you have lots of time. Stop waiting because the payoff is far away.

The Procrastination Doctor's Prescription: Move yourself out of freeze-frame by devoting just 10 minutes to the project. Make sure it is a focused, concentrated 10 minutes. Ask yourself questions. *What don't you know that you have to find out? What can't you do yourself? What do you need that must be bought?* These 10 minutes can allow you to sculpt a plan of action that can dissolve the need to use procrastination to hide a fear that comes from the bigness of a task or project. This stops procrastination cold and long enough to learn what has to happen before you can complete the project.

Which types of procrastination ring true for you? Can you spot the different types of procrastination in others you know?

Watch out for the double-standard that can keep you from seeing the big red barn of your procrastination. We tend to judge others by what they do and ourselves by our motivation or intention to act. So others only get points for producing while we give ourselves points for good intention. Try harvesting vegetables planted by good intentions.

Another double-standard sidetracks us from important tasks by keeping up with the easy, little tasks. The rationale becomes, *Oh, it only takes a minute to get this thing out of the way.* No one can fault you, after all you are working. Behind putting off the big things may be these fears of judgment, both yours and others':

- ❖ The finished job may not be acceptable.
- ❖ Criticism.
- ❖ Rejection.
- ❖ Changes required after completion.

Consider high-energy and low-energy as additional clues to discover yours and others' procrastination. The hardest procrastinators to recognize are the balls of fire, high-energy types, buried in busy-ness. These busy bees buzz from task to task. Lack of focus and goal orientation keeps them from progress, however. They look so busy, others are afraid to ask them to take on any more. That works fine for these over-organized whirlwinds who can't commit to the important tasks long enough to finish them.

The Procrastination Doctor's Prescription: Track your time, prioritize task collaboratively in the beginning until you can make and stick to realistic schedules. Learn to rise above mistakes, because they happen to focused, productive people. Try doubling the time you estimate a task to take. You can usually move up a schedule easier than you can push it back, especially when you are engaged in team efforts. Avoid particularly getting trapped by what comes along to distract you, both externally and internally. Except for real emergencies, stick to your schedule.

Wheel-spinning low-energy procrastinators are easier to spot. They analyze to paralysis, lose themselves in the positive and negative, and get little actually done. They often fear going out on a limb, taking risks. Wheel-spinners can talk an amazing project. With a focus on the big things, they may forget to do all the little things that make the big things a reality.

The Procrastination Doctor's Prescription: Wheel-spinners need to find a way that works for them to jump-start themselves with small tasks they can begin and finish quickly. They need a schedule that breaks down their barn-sized vision into first-things-first tasks. Then, they need a schedule that breaks tasks into time blocks that allow for preparation and cleanup. This plants the seeds of their vision in an environment where blooming becomes possible.

Both types of procrastinators can polish their commitment skills with small rewards throughout their projects with a bigger reward at the end. Honoring progress makes each success more real and makes continued success possible.

Regardless of profile or type, the prescription for procrastination centers around these three actions:

1. Setting Goals—prioritizing step-by-step what needs to be done and by when you need to do it
2. Doing Work—forcing yourself to do tasks in blocks of time every day
3. Rewarding Yourself—reinforcing the benefits of good habits by taking the time to physically honor your accomplishments

Goethe said, *Every . . . [one] has enough strength to complete those assignments that . . . [one] is fully convinced are important.*

Depression, Going Fallow

Within the context of this book, passive-aggressive/revenge depression can happen when an individual in a difficult relationship slips into depression to avoid the relationship and the person they blame for its problems. Depressed, they remove themselves from availability to a person they feel makes life miserable for them. Frustrated, without a solution, depression happens.

Recognize that passive-aggressive depression may be the smallest number among the depressed twenty million Americans. According to Michelle Healy, a writer for *USA Today*, the disorder will strike 1 in 5 women and 1 in 10 men over the course of their lifetimes. I discuss depression here to increase understanding and encourage dialogue, because depression is such a large, mostly hidden, problem in our society. Shame, cost, and embarrassment keep the suffering and depressed away from the treatment that helps 90 percent of those who seek it.

Much seems to be written about chemical imbalance depression overcome by the right magic pill. Yet, only one person I spoke with took a prescription drug. Without her daily pill she was suicidal; with it she was not. Hardly a cure.

What I personally know of depression pales against the complexity of the problem, and humbles me. When I interviewed the chronically depressed and those who overcame their depression, I was opened to an amazing world of tender caring for others, deep sadness within, and many forms of emotional struggles. They threw my black and white analogies back at me time and again and said, "It's just not that way for me."

Like candles in the wind, the depressed fight a constant battle to keep their sadness from blowing out their light. While negative self-talk plagues some, others had feelings more like an ominous ill wind blowing sadness round and round. Some knew no reason why they harbored such great sadness.

For most, their sadness ebbs and flows like a great crow that comes to eat at their corn of contentment. When the sadness strikes, the crow steals the moment. The battle is lost until the depressed can shoo it away, however long that takes. For those with bipolar depressive disorder, that could be many weeks of mental and emotional immobility.

While chemical imbalance may be diagnosed for some depressed individuals, more than 50 percent of depressed people never seek treatment for the inner turmoil they endure.

Again and again in speaking with the depressed, I found sad people with big, soft hearts. They care deeply about the suffering that goes on in the world. They have a melancholy about them, a hopelessness that includes the world at large.

The depressed can also be rigidly tough on themselves with near impossible expectations they keep trying to meet. Unlike the stereotypes bantered about regarding the depressed, many I interviewed push themselves terribly hard to do more, get better, gain more control, and get normal.

Despair became one of the common threads that found their way in the emotional tapestry of each of those I interviewed. Sadness and a hopeless fog were the others. They lack hope in a better tomorrow. They struggle with a hopelessness that there is nothing better out there, a feeling that nothing is ever going to change. Several toggle between feeling optimistic and pessimistic, yet admit to more pessimism. Getting to optimistic was a push.

Moving in and out of their states of depression, many of the depressed function fairly well. Time and again, I heard, *You could work with a depressed person and never know the things they fight inside of themselves every day.* The battle they fight is constant. They don't want to let the sadness eat away at them their whole entire life. Many keep working on gaining control every day, trying to make things better, involving themselves in self-improvement activities, and volunteering. Some pray a lot.

The depressed I interviewed felt only a small minority openly show their depression. They believed most depressed people keep their depression to themselves. When their depression got bad, many said they went through periods where they slept a lot, like they couldn't seem to get enough sleep. Others couldn't sleep. Many ate and ate. Others couldn't eat.

None of the people I interviewed agreed with the common description of depression as anger turned inward. What they feel is hopeless, choiceless, and they despair.

I've also seen mental hold describe severe depression, which keeps people from experiencing active and engaging lives. The deeply depressed can seem like people on mute, no picture, no sound, suspended in sadness. Early on, in the interviews, it became clear that most of them fight hard to keep above deep depression.

The depressed said they did what they had to do, saw to their responsibilities, kept their lives together. They smiled, conversed, joked, stayed engaged, all to hide their depression from others.

Some felt guilt, anxiety, and shame. Others stressed only the sadness to the core of their beings and the despair they fight on a daily basis.

When you make efforts to understand the illness of depression, recognize that there are levels of depression as well as time frames. Since most depressed people work hard to hide their depression from others, having a working knowledge about depression is important in maintaining and building relationships. Short-term depression, for example, touches nearly everyone.

Short-term, most likely situational, depression usually comes from a shock of some kind, death, terminated relationship, job loss, disease, illness, or accident.

Chronic depression can originate with situational depression and never go away, like those who don't recover from the loss of a child, parent, spouse, or lover. No matter how many times people tell them *Move on . . . Get over it . . . Get a life*—they can't.

Losing someone you love hurts. You feel physical stress, heartbreak, and physical loss. Your loss can never be replaced. The healthy go through the grief process and eventually move on. For others, loss triggers a fear of their own diminished life. The imagined loss of their own wholeness causes a free-floating loss that can never be resolved, leading them into chronic depression. Sometimes loss can trigger feelings about how good life used to be, and how they didn't appreciate the things someone did when they were with them. Part of the sadness involves wishing they could have some of those good times back.

The depressed can feel anxious, tense about their sad feelings taking over. When the depression gets bad, they are in a place walled off from happiness. The sadness has won temporarily. Moving back out of the sadness takes a great deal of effort.

I found little black and white or clear-cut about depression. Others rarely see what each depressed person goes through on a daily basis. How easy it is to write off the depressed population and label them as cop-outs who should just stop being depressed. Oh, if the solution were that easy.

When you empathize with the depressed you can't help but gain respect for their struggles. The depressed know most others do not understand. That's somewhat okay with the depressed in hiding. For others, it breaks their hearts, because they desperately want someone, anyone, to understand the awfulness of the way they feel. A dependent depressed person in hiding may be clinging to you for dear life and you may not know it. The depressed can also confound others with their moods, up/down, talkative/quiet, and engaged/disengaged. A controlling depressed person, for example, can waffle between being assertive and acting like a doormat. They've got so much turmoil going on inside, they can't deal with more coming at them from the outside. They give in to keep outside peace.

Healer Hannelore Christensen gave me this description of depression: *Try to imagine yourself in a room that is dark and foggy with no windows and doors. You can't see. You can't feel a way out. You don't know how you got there, because all of a sudden you're there. The depressed are in that foggy room that ranges from mild gray to utter blackness. They see no choices they can make to get out. They can't see any light. They see shadows instead of sunshine. The darkness catches them. They are in emotional limbo where they can't really act. Depression is like getting lost. You lose your focus. You need to find home, your center, again.*

In relationships, when dealing with a person you suspect suffers from depression, give them listening support, loving empathy, and genuine compassion. Most don't talk about the sadness inside. They just deal with it. Others are more out there with their depression and they do talk about it. Each depressed person is different. However, if their travails get repeated ad nauseum and/or begin taking up too much of your time, assert yourself matter-of-factly. *I am sorry you are still having trouble in your relationship and I need to take care of . . . I'll call you in a few days. I am sorry your situation hasn't changed and I'd rather talk about something else. Your job situation sounds frustrating. Do you have other job options?*

Some chronically depressed can get stuck lamenting what they no longer have, don't have, no longer can do, and can't do. This can happen after financial loss, physical and mental deterioration, from aging or illness. They focus on what they lack rather than what they have. And they can suffer from their profound feelings of deprivation.

When depression rages, they do lack. They lack some of the essential attitudes and character traits that generally make people happy. Faith, hope, love, and trust get lost to them during depression attacks. They may look at faith as something of a crutch and reject it. Rather, faith in God, someone or something can hold them together when nothing else can. The deeply depressed may lose hope because their attention focuses on the past where no amount of hope can change what already happened. They can struggle with loving themselves unconditionally and, therefore, struggle also to love others without expectation. Love with conditions feels demanding. Each condition feels like a stab in sore and hurting hearts. Trust is also hard for the deeply depressed. Trust is a spiritual strength that requires people to suspend disbelief about themselves, others, and life. Trust says I believe in me, you, and life, even though I can't tell you how or why. Trust lets go and lets God or whatever name you give to spiritual strength. Trust is a knowing and sometimes the sadness blocks out the quiet voice of intuition or inner knowing.

Instead of intuition, some depressed may have doubting minds, filled with negative thoughts voiced by their inner critic that constantly questions the self, assigns blame and places guilt. With school finished, the doubting mind may attack the young. With work finished, the doubting mind may attack prime-timers. With child-rearing finished, the doubting mind may attack empty-nesters.

Depression, then, becomes an obsession with the negative, what went wrong in their lives, what could go wrong, and how every personality fault of theirs is far worse then anyone else's. They are afraid their carefully constructed emotional dam will self-destruct at any minute. They live on the emotional edge, feel exposed, emotionally naked in a mental world where emotional control is prized.

From seeds planted by the doubting mind can come a dissatisfaction with the self, a dislike. In doubt and dislike of self, some depressed people avoid quiet and being alone. Aloneness forces their sadness upon them. Noise distracts, so the television may be on at the same time radio earplugs fight their mental static directly.

Several of the depressed I interviewed told me they couldn't relate to the mental static or the need for noise. Some liked being alone, needed quiet to concentrate. Others weren't aware of any feelings of dislike of self.

Some depressed people may develop odd ways of looking at life. Bogged down by past hurts, they seem to be hoping yesterday will get better. They worry. And they miss out on the pleasures and opportunities of today. In the middle of a family gathering, amid the talking, laughing, and love, one depressed person desperately fought tears. All she could think of was: *This is all going to be over soon.*

Some depressed, therefore, suffer also from the Should Disease, or Hardening of the Oughteries. They lament shoulda's, coulda's, woulda's, if only's. Since a mind can't be in two places at once, wallowing in what-if's stops the depressed from experiencing the now, the only place where better things can happen.

Other depressed seriously seek connection, want to feel like they belong to someone or something. They want to stop feeling like outsiders looking in on life. Yet, their emotional preoccupation can push others away. The very people they want to connect with can find them detached, cold, aloof, even rude and unfeeling. That's the opposite of the way most are. Instead they feel so much, care so much, and they are afraid to let it all come out.

Some depressed feel they are paying dearly for their seats in the big arena of life and life gives them bad seats or sometimes none at all. As depression lingers, life becomes harder and harder, and some become difficult to be around. Those who are open about their depression can look mopey, complain about their terrible life, force smiles, have a hard time paying attention in conversation, and find it difficult to talk about anything but themselves.

Other depressed suffer from inside-out thinking. They can spend too much time trying to control people, situations, places, and things outside themselves. They lose sight of the fact that they are the only person they have control over. Give some depressed people a magic genie and their wishes would most likely be to change others: *I wish my partner would be more loving. I wish my mother would stop criticizing me. I wish my boss would appreciate what I do.*

Curing chronic depression can begin with the depressed learning their terrible feelings have a name, *depression.* After the understanding that they suffer from something that is highly treatable and curable, the depressed can find their way back into living with a spark of confidence, a glimmer of faith.

People have said these things about their depressions:

Young Married Mother of Three—I felt so ugly, useless, and worthless. I got to the point where I hated the way I looked so much I didn't even want to wash or comb my hair. I just wanted to die, but I couldn't kill myself. I realized if something didn't change soon, I'd go crazy. I thought I'd reached bottom until going crazy became a possibility. That's when I went on the diet and took up hairdressing. I wish I'd done this years ago. I'm having fun for the first time in my life!

The Minority Corporate Executive—I don't want to be here. I never wanted to be here. I don't feel like I belong here. I've felt alone on this planet as long as I can remember.

The Homeless Single Parent—I just felt so horribly, horribly sad, guilty for all the awful things I've done, and I just wanted to end the pain of being me. Then God rescued me, and I know I'll never go to that terrible place again.

The College Professor—I am unipolar. I exercise, do what I can. When I wake up depressed, I try exercise to see if I can break it. If not, I stay home, clean up things, file, read. It would be career suicide for anyone to see me this way. Look, sometimes it can be convenient. If something is coming up that I don't want to deal with, I can wake up depressed. Who knows if I brought it on or not. What I do know is, if I can't snap myself out of it, I go nowhere.

The Retired Country Housewife—When I was in the hospital all those weeks, people were waiting on me, taking care of me. I had a lot of time to think. I realized I had been depressed for years. I made up my mind to just stop all the worrying about what this one thinks and what that one is going to do. Life's too short. As soon as I got stronger, I cleaned up the house, got some new clothes, and I stopped being a silent doormat. Now I speak up. If I want something I get it. And I'm finally going to do something about all this weight. It's ridiculous. I'm five foot tall and almost as wide.

Single Mother—I just feel so sad all the time. Deep down I don't feel like I deserve anything too good. Somehow when bad things happen to me, I feel like I deserve them. I feel so bad about all the things I've done, so ashamed, so unforgivable.

At some point, a number of the depressed get out from under by making a simple decision to stop suffering. When they make that decision, they seem to be able to see how they deny themselves pleasure. They stop trying to win over people they don't really like, who aren't nice to them, and who constantly criticize them.

Some are able to reach out to God and pray their way out. Others surround themselves with the beautiful and they get out. Many get out with the help of somebody who cares enough to help them out. Still others get out with professional help and medicine.

They move from denying themselves pleasure to a motto that says, *I deserve, too.*

To heal, the depressed must go inside and muck around mentally to process their sadness. They need to cognitively experience their inner world of emotions.

From mental clearing, many depressed need to move on to physical clearing. Long stuck in their mental quicksand, those coming out of depression need to fix their appearances, spruce up their wardrobes, clean out their cars, residences, and offices.

Many depressed, however, function at high levels and have no more than normal needs to keep down clutter and spruce up periodically. They suffer in silence, behind closed doors, inside, where no one can see their pain.

Somewhere into the healing process, the depressed benefit from a healthy sense of humor that allows them to laugh at themselves and their illogical self-defeating behaviors.

I cut this Anti-Depression Kit out of a newsletter and shared it with those I interviewed. Some found it really funny and wanted one; others hated it, thought it was stupid and trivialized a terrible problem.

Anti-Depression Kit

An eraser	so you can make all your troubles disappear
A rubber band	to stretch yourself beyond your limits
A penny	so you never need to say you are broke
A string	to tie things together when everything falls apart
A marble	in case someone says you have lost all of yours
Hugs & kisses	to remind you that someone, somewhere cares

Laughter keeps people emotionally flexible, softens the pain of sadness, and soothes the hurts so the depressed can win more battles with the sadness, move on quicker when depression hits, and stop getting stuck.

Depression, however, is no laughing matter. The chronically depressed fight a valiant daily battle with the sadness that torments them. They bravely function in spite of their inner turmoil, and work hard to get better. They taught me and taught me. I learned to love every one of them as they opened their hearts to me. I hope what they taught me can help you understand depression when someone in your life, or you, gets caught up in it.

HARVEST SUMMARY FOR CHAPTER 2: DROUGHT, EMOTIONS THAT HARDEN HEARTS

PLANTING GOOD SEEDS IN FERTILE SOIL

Who you are grows the kind of life you have. Here you learn to use the tools you need to "Grow Yourself a Life You"ll Love."

Decide you want a different life? Then, you must create a different you. As long as you believe the same things, carry around the same attitudes, and behave the same way, you are going to get the same life. Change yourself—change your life.

When you bring your new you to your relationships, your relationships will change, as well. Empathy enables you to get yourself out of the way of others' messages. Body language lets you read between others' words, so when you decide what you want to say, you bring insights into your conversations not available to the self-centered.

In those times when your communications hit ruts and rocks, despite your efforts, you learn to rely on a positive attitude and a sense of humor to fill in the emotional lows and push the rocks out of the way.

PART TWO

Chapter 3

Self Is Seed for the Life You Lead

Introduction

Once you go inside yourself and poke around, you'll find you are the most exciting, enticing mystery you will ever know. The journey of self-discovery amazes and agonizes, sometimes all at once. Never boring, you'll discover you're more than you ever thought possible.

You'll find yourself paying more attention to what you say and do, because whatever you do lasts forever. Here's one story:

> A single father's two children had terrible tempers. They groused at each to her, stomped and stormed about the house, and frequently got into trouble at school.
>
> Worried they would one day hurt each other or someone else, the father called his children into his

> study and handed each one a plate with two large thick-skinned potatoes along with a box of nails.
>
> He told them, "Now, each time you lose your temper I want you to push a nail into one potato, leaving the other potato nail free. When you go one whole day without losing your temper once, come back to me."
>
> Days went by as the children went frequently in and out of their father's study, until one day the girl came to him and said, "Daddy, I didn't lose my temper once today."
>
> He told her, "Okay, now start pulling a nail out of your potato for every day you hold your temper in check."
>
> Soon the boy too was pulling nails out.
>
> One day, the children came to the study and said, "Look, daddy, all the nails are out of our potatoes!"
>
> "Well, children, I'm proud of you. You've learned that you can choose whether or not to lose your temper when you get angry. But now I want you to look at your two potatoes. One is healthy and its skin is unbroken. Now look at the other potato, all full of hurts. That's how your anger leaves people, all full of hurts. Remember these potatoes the next time your temper flares up and you want to push your anger at someone."

Your big and little questions day in and day out determine the quality of your life and the imprint you make on others' lives. The big questions: *Who am I? Who am I with? What do I stand for? What do I stand against? What is the meaning of my life? Could I learn to love unconditionally?* The little questions: *What is the lesson for me in this trouble? Is there an opportunity I'm not seeing? How does the other person see this situation? How have I helped create this problem? How do I show my gratitude to others? Could I look first for the good instead of the bad?*

In *Letters to a Young Poet,* Rainer Maria Rilke wrote: *Be patient toward all that is unresolved in your heart. Try to love the questions themselves. . . . Live the questions now.*

You are the master gardener of your life. If you want to become happy and stay happy, you need to take the initiative to ask yourself the questions to grow a life you'll love living, in glorious wonder, fully in love with your future.

e.e. cummings said, *To be nobody but yourself in a world which is doing its best to make you everybody else means to fight the hardest battle which any human being can fight and never stop fighting.*

In trying to understand what makes you do the things you do, I've developed a Behavior Cycle Model. Here's how it works:

Premise 1—Your biases determine your attitudes.

Premise 2—Your attitudes determine your feelings.

Premise 3—Your feelings drive you to act.

Action arises out of choice. If you want a good life, you need to make good choices. Simply stated, how you think about something determines how you feel about it, which determines what you do. When you train yourself to think positively, you tend to make more positive choices.

Who you are results from two basic systems, your belief system and your value system. Together they create your character.

Your Behavior Cycle Model comes directly from your beliefs, attitudes, and feelings. Then you act out of choice. When you believe that other people or your environment causes any of them, you have chosen to give away control of your life. You have freely chosen to let other people and other things push your buttons.

When we understand ourselves we are clear about our beliefs and values. When we don't, we become adults living out childhood biases. For example, at home, my mother worried constantly about my workaholic father. *What good is making all this money if you're half-dead and can't enjoy it?* As a child I learned to believe that making a lot of money was a bad thing. As an adult that belief turned into a fear of success that held me down until I dug and dug inside to understand what blocked my financial success. When I found the story behind the block, I could change my belief about money. Now, within my new belief context that money, neither good nor bad, buys opportunities, it enables me to be free to earn without limit.

Each of our cherished biases has a story behind it. Some stories are positive and some, like the one above, limit us. When you encounter defensiveness, fear of making mistakes, doubt, and anxiety that eat away at your self-confidence, erode your self-esteem, dig for the belief and the story behind it.

You will then see how certain behaviors happen as if on automatic pilot. Your underlying subconscious belief system kicks in and you act without thought. While you don't consciously remember the story behind the belief, your subconscious mind can't forget the programming. Consider this extreme example of abuse victims who have benevolent amnesia. An event so terrible, to remember it consciously would create trauma, so they spare themselves that. But the programming remains. So a child rape victim fears those of the same sex as the rapist.

How you behave comes from what you believe. Your level of self-respect tells you your worth, your level of self-confidence what you can do, and your self-responsibility what you own up to. That's why it is so important to keep aware of these and protect them from being lowered. Like plants, self-respect, self-confidence, and self-responsibility need constant watering to keep them alive and growing. They are fragile. Time and again I've seen an abusive boss, spouse, lover, parent, friend, sibling suck the life out of a vibrant individual over a short period of time. It can happen. It does happen. When you don't pay attention, all of a sudden, like depression, you're there, disabled.

Watch groveling for approval which can become your Achilles' heel. Before you declare you never grovel, consider that giving in too often is a type of groveling. There is more to giving in than keeping the peace; there is also avoiding conflict. People naturally want approval, to be liked, loved, and that is not groveling. However, you need to understand you must be willing to risk being disliked if you want to be loved. Authenticity says, "I am true to myself 100 percent of the time. I don't engage in buffers, filters, and other false people-fooling behaviors made up for the moment." The submissive and dependent wear a love mask. These individuals fail to take responsibility for their own lives. The aggressive and controlling wear a power mask. These people act selfishly, demanding things their way. The fearful and insecure wear a cordial mask to hide the turmoil inside. In denial, these individuals refuse to face and deal with life in a timely manner.

The many masks of false personality hide grief, hate, rage, fear, shame, and guilt. These are ugly feelings we don't want to show and spoil our carefully protected nice image. These negative feelings box us into hiding part of ourselves.

When you are a people-pleaser, you play to the person you're with, act differently around different people. When you act differently around each person, who are you really? My mother's adage, *The truth will out*, unmasks false faces eventually. One single truth overcomes 900 lies. Think how unfair it is to lead someone to believe you are one way when you really are another. Can you see how they would feel betrayed and angry when they find out?

Authenticity takes courage and commitment. You accept that some people won't like you. To achieve authenticity, you must integrate two You's. One You comes from what you actually say and do, your behavior, and is the You others see. The second You comes from your motivations and intentions and is the You you know. When your intentions and your actions match, you achieve authenticity. When they don't, you create confusion.

The four-pane Johari Window shows you who you are. The upper left window speaks of the common part of yourself that others and you know. The upper right speaks to your blind spot, what others know about you that you don't know. The bottom right speaks to the part of yourself that you purposely hide from others. The bottom left speaks to the part of you that nobody knows, our most mysterious part.

Consider only one part out of four represents information known by others and us. People, on average, know only fifty percent about themselves. As much as seventy-five percent of our personalities can confuse others and us. I developed Character Architectural Technology℠ to help clear up a good deal of the mystery we are to others and ourselves. While the complete system forms the subject of an upcoming book, I include the foundation of the system here.

People use three universal Thinking Styles to understand the world—Intuitive, Cerebral, and Emotional—but tend to depend too heavily on one, their default. View the human understanding mechanism as a three-headed giant. One head holds the instincts that tell us what to do. Another contains the control machinery that tells us how to do it. The other holds the feelings that tell us why to do it.

In my studies of personality, I found several of the great philosophers discussed personality, Plato and Aristotle among them. Head, Heart, and Gut intelligences go back hundreds of years. My Intuitive, Cerebral, and Emotional Thinking Styles are mirrors of that vein of thought.

There is also biological grounding for this time-honored head, heart, gut system. We are three-brained beings. Body smart is connected to the reptilian or physical brain. Head smart is connected to the neocortex or rational brain. Heart smart is connected to the limbic (also called the mammalian) or emotional brain.

You have a preferred way of thinking, taking in and giving out information, and others have a style preference as well. Can you imagine what occurs when you expect others to mirror your style? It can be like speaking German to a Russian. Yet, each Thinking Style is equally important in communicating. You can change your life when you open yourself up to the other two styles of thinking. Then, you are capable of speaking Russian when you converse with Russians.

The Three Thinking Styles, Intuitive, Cerebral, and Emotional, are available to everyone. Freely flexing among the three remains an elusive goal for most. So, people favor their preferred style. What works about a favorite style? Comfort and skill. What doesn't work? Inappropriate method in certain situations. When you are in danger, you need to go with your gut and get away. You waste precious time in Cerebral considering all the ways to get away or in Emotional worrying about how everyone else can get away, too. Sound selfish? Let me ask you what good you can be to anyone if you don't get away?

Each of the Thinking Styles represents a personal method of processing information. Here, you'll see some generalities framed in comparison. The Intuitives, action-oriented, focus on acting on what needs to be done and doing it. These body-smart people I nickname the Gear-Shift Decision-Makers, who quickly get into gear and go. The Cerebrals, information-oriented, focus on meanings and understanding how things fit together. These head-smart people I nickname Pool Table Decision-makers, who look at all the possibilities before they act. The Emotionals, people-oriented, want to know how decisions will affect people. These heart-smart people I nickname Personal Chef Decision-Makers, trying to please as many people as possible and offend as few people as possible.

What generally happens when the three styles don't get their way? Intuitives get aggressive. Cerebrals withdraw. Emotionals give in. Each style can become enraged, however, and lose control.

The three universal Thinking Styles are actually three parts of a whole. When the three work together, the Intuitives give input as to what to do; the Cerebrals process the input and provide the how-to's for each of the what's; and the Emotionals provide the energy to actually do the what's.

When you understand all three universal Thinking Styles, you can avoid needless conflict. When you recognize not only your preferred Thinking Style, but also others', you are in a much better position to understand others and make yourself understood, as well. Your communication becomes user-friendly, more natural.

This comparison shows the differences among the Thinking Styles:

Intuitive	**Cerebral**	**Emotional**
How Am I?	Where Am I?	Who Am I With?
Voice Of Will	Voice Of Reason	Voice Of Heart
Sense, Feel, Do	Process, Feel, Do	Connect, Feel, Do
Control	Security	Approval
Decision-Maker	Problem-Solver	Image-Maker
The What	The How	The Who
Creative	Careful	Caring
Finish	Begin	Build Onto
Truth	Understanding	Love

Can you look at this comparison of the three Thinking Styles and know which one you are? If not, can you look and know which one you definitely are not?

If you compare your Thinking Style to the foundation of a building, personality would be the first floor.

Beyond the foundation of the universal Thinking Styles, my Character Architecture Technology℠ system delves into personality. Beginning with a personal growth model that includes the Thinking Styles there follows a number of personal behavior preferences that make up who we are as individuals.

From the seeds planted by your biological parents, you grow your personality based on how the world treats you, what you learn, and what you find you like and dislike. You'll learn the nine preferences I believe are inherited and some of the other preference choices that influence personality. Then, you'll find common personality preferences you will carry throughout your life unless you choose to change them:

- ❖ Type A or Type B Energy
- ❖ Private/Introverted or Public/Extroverted Personality
- ❖ Left Brain or Right Brain Orientation

Next, you'll find seven types of difficult people. Then, you'll learn 27 qualities people like about others along with six qualities of the charismatic personality. After that, you'll wander with me into the secret depths of your subconscious mind.

Finally, you will see the role self-discipline plays in your efforts to effect change. Here, you'll learn concepts like *time quickening* and *fake it until you make it.* More importantly, you'll learn to stop putting up with the things that drag you down, whether they are your own bad habits, others' problems, or adverse environmental effects.

Said Ben Franklin, *Dost thou love life? Then do not squander time, for that's the stuff life is made of.*

Personality, Varieties and Colors

Julian Huxley says, *During . . . [one's] growth, mere individuality becomes personality, and the developed individual personality is not only the most complex type of organization known, and one which exhibits a far greater range of diversity among its members than any other single type of organization, but the highest product of evolution of which we have any knowledge.*

I say, *Our personality is the result of behaviors we have favored and traits and characteristics we have developed either consciously or unconsciously.*

Out of your familial, cultural, geographic, and environmental mythologies you craft a personal mythology, or a system of beliefs that underlie your actions. From the basic aspects of personality—physical, mental, spiritual, and emotional—I searched for something concrete that made sense to my workshop participants and clients. Grounded in the bodies of research of Piaget, Erikson, and Vygotsky, I wrote my master's thesis on how young children develop. Each seminar, *Gee, Some People Have a Funny Way of Looking at Things,* begins with a developmental foundation chart that shows Stage One as Conception. At Stage Two, we are born into Physical Reality with nature-based tendencies or temperaments.

Stages of Development

One — Conception

Two — Physical Reality

Three — Awareness

Four — Relationships

Five — Communication

Six — Language

Seven — Beliefs and Concepts

Eight — Individuality

Nine — Being/Essence

After research and, particularly, watching babies grow, I believe we inherit these personality traits as natural tendencies:

- ❖ Aggressive or Submissive
- ❖ Leader or Follower
- ❖ High Energy or Laid Back
- ❖ Active Imagination or Limited Exercise of Imagination
- ❖ Skill in Language or Difficulty Expressing Self
- ❖ Friendly (Extrovert) or Shy (Introvert)
- ❖ Strong Will or Weak Will
- ❖ Like Change/Risk Taker or Like Tradition/Risk Averse
- ❖ Generous or Selfish

Modern science now supports the claim that our personalities are formed more by nature than by nurture.

In the beginning of stage two we notice hunger or satiation, warmth or cold, and comfort or discomfort. After several months, at Stage Three, we begin awareness of Conditions and Circumstances, and develop the beginnings of our Problem-Solving Style: Aggressive or Dependent or Withdrawing. Next, at Stage Four, we form Relationships, know our parents/caregivers, because we now understand that we are separate from the adults who care for us. At this stage, we understand that some things are ours.

My daughter Karen-Marie, before age two, standing in her playpen, called me over to her. She began, one by one, picking up each toy and saying to me, "Mine!" She looked to me for collaboration, and I gave it to her. When she had gone through every toy in her playpen, she pointed to me and said, "Mine!" And I answered her, "Yours and your sister, Vicky's." On hearing my answer, she burst into loud wailing.

Stage Five, Communication, coincides with the first signs of a preference for one of three Coping/Stress Reaction Styles: Proactive, Negotiating, and Reactive. Then comes the Stage Six, Language. Sentences come more often. Curiosity and new learning broaden vocabulary. With the rapid acquiring of mental and physical knowledge comes the Stage Seven, the formation of Beliefs and Concepts, and a preference for a personality type. Between ages four and seven, some behaviors become predictable by caregivers and teachers. At the Stage Eight, we develop our Individuality. Lastly, at Stage Nine, if we work on personal growth, we confront our demons and return to our Being, or Essence, innocent and uncontaminated. We become truly spiritual beings, living in the present moment, unhindered by past baggage, living fully in the present moment, knowing God.

By age four, we have made some important decisions about ourselves. Generally, we have an opinion about whether we are good or bad, whether our world is a safe or scary place. From total dependence, we find some modicum of independence. We test our caregivers with no's and I won'ts. Often we identify with the messages our parents or caregivers give us. Unfortunately, these opinions are largely unconscious ones.

By age forty, some people experience, sometimes in horror that they have become much like their parents. They hear themselves say the same things to their children that they hated hearing from their parents. When they realize it, they wonder how it happened when they vowed never to be like that. One woman told the story of how she looked in the mirror one morning and saw her mother's face looking back at her. Shocked, she said, "What are you doing in my mirror?" She laughs now when she tells the story, but she quickly adds that it wasn't one bit funny when it happened.

During our lifetimes, I believe our environment teaches us optimism or pessimism, trust or suspicion, and strong success drive or weak success drive. And these I believe change as our inner or outer environment changes.

All during our lives, we acquire unconscious imprints. I feel a strong case can be made for these unconscious imprints leading both men and women to midlife crises when they wonder who they are and why they don't particularly like their lives or who they realize they have become. Sometimes they seek a scapegoat to blame, their job, their spouse, their parents, or others in their circle of influence. They abruptly leave jobs or stop doing good work, leave relationships, sometimes rushing into a wild lifestyle. Sometimes it seems as if they are trying to wind their clocks back to twenty again to start a better future than they made for themselves the first time around. Some succeed in creating new lives for themselves, others fail horribly. The most successful group are those who aim for personal growth through change, self-discipline, and self-management. They frequently ask themselves questions: *Who am I? What am I about? What is the meaning of my life?*

It's horrible when you feel afraid that your life will end before you do anything worthwhile. A commitment to self-introspection can help you discover the meaning of your life. Working through your fear can make fear your friend. It functions as a wake-up call. Out of the fear, you get the opportunity to explore, learn, and grow. The fear forces you to look at how you came to be the way you are. How are you like your parents? Do you want to keep on being that way? What are your beliefs? Where did they come from? Are they still true for you, or do you need to change them to get where you want to go? Look at choices. Have they created a good life for you? If not, how can you make better choices and create a better life?

Along the way to adulthood, you have developed behavioral preferences. Behavioral styles or preferences are neither good nor bad. They just exist. When you squeeze an orange, you get orange juice. If you expected tomato juice, you're in for a disappointment. When you understand these preferences are comparable to orange juice from oranges, you won't expect public people to keep their business to themselves or private people to discuss their personal business. Let's look at comparative charts of some of the preferences.

TYPE A	**TYPE B**
Proactive	Reactive
Moves quickly	Moves at an easy pace
Eats fast	Eats more slowly and relaxes
Speaks quickly	Speaks slowly
Impatient	Patient
Aggressive, easily upset	Laid back, easygoing
Competitive	Cooperative
Pressured for time	Unhurried
Seeks satisfaction	Finds satisfaction
Uptight	Relaxed
Does several things at once	Does one thing at a time
Questions to challenge	Questions to clarify
Shares opinions	Reserves opinions

PRIVATE PERSONALITY/ Introvert	**PUBLIC PERSONALITY/ Extrovert**
Intrapersonal	Interpersonal
Avoids conflict	Resolves conflict
Concept-oriented	People-oriented
Thinks things through	Talks things out
Drawn to inner world of ideas	Drawn to outer world of people

Recharges energy alone	Recharges energy around people
Comes to conclusions alone	Dialogues to reach conclusions
Finds writing easier than talking	Finds talking easier than writing
Direct and blunt	Softens hard statements
Strong conscience	Tends to rationalize

LEFT BRAIN	**RIGHT BRAIN**
Favors logic and reason	Favors intuition and creativity
Life ordered and controlled	Life spontaneous and flexible
Identifies with individual	Identifies with group
Analyzes and takes apart	Synthesizes and puts together
Thinks in words	Thinks in pictures
Thinks sequentially	Thinks simultaneously
Sees the trees	Sees the forest
Builds a case when angry	Generalizes/evades when angry

Beyond behavioral styles, some people you deal with are just plain difficult.

Gossips—They tattle and tell stories about everybody and everything, mostly negative. Usually gossip seeks to build the gossip up or tear the subject of the gossip down. Three tactics work to stop gossip: avoid doing it; refuse to listen to it; and ask for support of gossip's statements.

Know-It-Alls—These experts exasperate, try everyone's patience, even when they are right. Sometimes the best tactic is humor and exaggeration. Most know-it-alls really believe they know, think they are being helpful, and believe they are educating you and others with their proclamations.

Non-Stop Talkers—These people can be know-it-alls or just needy people who want to be heard. Again, humor and exaggeration can sometimes help.

Pessimists—These naysayers are everywhere. Sneeze and they say you are coming down with a cold. Humor can help you stay positive. There is a custom 'round the world where people say "God bless you" whenever anyone sneezes. I rather like that custom. When pessimists see something frustrating happen, they say you are having a bad day. Sometimes simple denial retains perspective, *I don't believe that, instead I feel my day is fine even though I have this problem.*

Put-Down Jokers—Nasty remarks with an *only kidding* tag line make fun of people and things. Call these mean-spirited people on their terrible habit, *I don't think your remark about me one bit funny.* Commonly, they retort with a sneer, *Oh, come on, can't you take a joke?* Call them again, *taking your jokes means putting up with your thinly disguised put-downs. Can't you make a joke that doesn't make fun of me that I can enjoy?*

Liars—Liars destroy others' trust and rightfully so. Lies make recipients feel foolish. When you suspect someone is lying to you, share your doubts specifically and factually.

Saboteurs—While fewer in number than other difficult people, these are the most destructive in relationships. Their dirty deeds are purposely disguised, hidden behind the scenes, planned and meant to hurt others. You have to really pay attention to catch these clever connivers. Rehabilitating them may be more than you need to take on. Move out of the relationship if you can. If not, factually confront, stating how the behavior interferes with your relationship.

Challenging difficult people's unacceptable behavior challenges you because some of the motivation for the bad behavior may come out of the unconscious, the part of their minds that contain automatic programming. Their beliefs locked within their subconscious minds sometimes control their motivation. Some truly don't see their behavior as difficult. The subconscious acts as puppeteer with the conscious mind acting as the puppet. Its automatic programming takes over when people lazily fail to put conscious thought into actions they take. Obviously, the mean-spirited are a different story, best out of your life, if possible.

Be watchful. Automatic programming can trip you up at any time, working against even your most focused hard work.

I came from Sicilian heritage on my father's side. When I was a small child and frustrated, I bit my hand until deep teeth marks formed. My mother, of course, told me to stop doing that, and eventually I did. Decades later, after a debilitating accident, insurance companies refused to pay valid claims in a timely manner. Debt load driving me into financial ruin, I discovered myself biting my hand. In instant flashback, I connected to my childhood action. What a curiosity, I formed a habit of biting my hand in frustration when I had never seen anyone do that before or since. Then seven years later, I heard comedian Loretta LaRoche speak of her Sicilian grandmother's Sicilian Warrior Stance, complete with hand biting. Was my childhood frustration response primal, passed through my gene pool, DNA, or some other blood connection to my father's ancestry? Certainly a possibility. Definitely an argument for nature rather than nurture as the architect of at least some aspects of our personalities.

Obviously, no one likes the behaviors of difficult people described above, but what behaviors do people like? From my workshop participants come 27 qualities they mention workshop after workshop:

Committed
Compassionate
Confident
Courageous
Decisive—clear about likes and dislikes
Dedicated
Determined
Express thoughts clearly
Fun
Generous
Goal-oriented

Honest
Intelligent
Nonjudgmental
Nurturing
Patient
Positive attitude
Reliable
Respects all people
Responsible
Trustworthy
Sense of humor
Sensitive to others
Smiles a lot
Spiritually connected
Straight forward
Willing to do whatever it takes

Along with correcting your difficult behaviors, you need to acquire and strengthen relationship-building behaviors. Here are seven behaviors that together create a charismatic personality:

Self-Discipline—The ability to be the true master of your fate, consciously in charge of body, mind, and spirit. (More this Chapter)

Positive Attitude—The skill to look for the good in all, appreciate life's blessings, and enjoy life's beauty. (More Chapter 5)

Sense of Humor—Laughter is the other side of tears and balances the heart. (More Chapter 5)

Honesty—The authentic person tells you true, behaves consistently, listens to the voice of conscience, and keeps promises.

Good Manners—Politeness, graciousness, courtesy, consideration all come under the umbrella of harmonious behavior toward others.

Empathy—The ability to understand others from their point of view is more compassionate than sympathy and kinder than pity. (More Chapter 4)

Service—The desire and commitment to give of self to make a difference in the world we inhabit. (More Chapter 5)

Here is the model for our behaviors. Our actions grow out of the three chambers of our mind: conscious, subconscious, and superconscious. The conscious mind finds life as it believes life to be, fitting the expression, *We see things as we are, rather than as they really are.* The subconscious becomes an obedient robot our conscious mind programs during our lifetime. It cannot tell the difference between what really happens and what we imagine. And it runs like a computer, good in/good out, garbage in/garbage out. The superconscious mind contains the seeds of our greatness. Some of us grow them and others do not. Stephen Hawkings, the nuclear physicist some acclaim as today's Einstein, cultivates his seeds, as did Helen Keller before him, with incredible passion. Both grew their seeds of greatness in their superconscious minds despite tremendous physical challenges.

Peter Senge said, "Where there is a genuine vision, people excel and learn, not because they are told to, but because they want to."

How sad when people die with their seeds of greatness dormant, depriving the world of the harvest only they can create out of their individual uniqueness.

You need the information in your subconscious mind, but how do you get it when the subconscious mind and the conscious mind can't communicate directly with each other? Meditation is one way, dreams and drugs are others. Since drugs are dangerous, not everyone meditates while everyone dreams, dreams become the information source I explore here.

The unconscious self reveals its secrets in the land of dreams where memories, repressed incidents, and denied feelings live.

Dreams teach, haunt, frighten, and help you to get to the root of your discontent. There are some helpful guidelines to harvest your dreams in a healthy way. First, be a traveler in your dreams rather than merely a tourist. The difference? Tourists take their home country wherever they go, comparing, measuring, judging, and seeking the familiar. Travelers understand *when in Rome, do as the Romans do.* They enter dreamland with an open heart, mind, and spirit. Travelers risk letting go of what they now know for the gifts of new insights. New insights make change possible. In dreams your hidden subconscious speaks to you. And it is your subconscious that has all the information. Compare the conscious and the subconscious minds. The conscious mind does one thing at a time. Even though you may do ten things in five minutes, you still do them one at a time. Your subconscious simultaneously takes in air, circulates blood, regulates body temperature, digests food, absorbs and distributes nourishment, hydrates skin, grows cells, nails, and hair, all without thought.

One dream showed me traveling with a group to a train station. Then, all of them disappeared and it seemed as if I might have missed the train. There I stood perplexed, wondering how it could have happened. Instead of trying to analyze the dream literally, I tried analyzing it emotionally. How did I feel? Lost, confused, abandoned, disconnected. Now, I look at my life and search for areas where I feel these things. Until I had the dream insight I would have had no reason to look.

Consider using dreams to work on personality traits you want to acquire, those you want to overcome, or problems you want to conquer.

Here are some guidelines:

Give Your Subconscious Mind A Particular Challenge Before You Go To Sleep. *Tell me what's at the bottom of my procrastination about writing my book.*

Record Your Dreams. Your dreams leave you as quickly as the name of a new person if you don't do something quick to retain them. Have a pad and paper right next to your bed to write your dream even before you go to the bathroom. (If you can't remember your dreams, try waking up earlier than usual to catch them.)

Analyze Your Dreams Creatively. Keep your challenge uppermost in your mind while looking for clues to an answer you can use. Remember the three Thinking Styles. Analyze your dreams intuitively, cerebrally, and emotionally. Intuitively you can mind map where you put a dream image in a circle, brainstorm all spontaneous thoughts, and write them down without judgment. Cerebrally you can look for patterns, fit, and connections. Emotionally you can look at the feelings that come up during the dream.

The key to developing an agreeable personality stems from paying attention to your interactions in relationships. No one seems to know who wrote this helpful guide:

Watch your thoughts; they become words.

Watch your words; they become actions.

Watch your actions, they become habits.

Watch your habits; they become character.

Watch your character; it becomes your destiny.

Change, Hybrid Vigor

American author, Christopher Morley said, "There is one success—to be able to spend your life in our own way." The sum total of the quality of your life comes from all the choices you make. Always there is choice in the beliefs you hold, the attitudes you exhibit, the feelings that come up, and the ultimate actions you choose to take. Even choosing not to act and acting as others wish for you to act represent your choice to relinquish your power to act.

The poem, *The Man in the Glass,* of unknown authorship, speaks to responsibility and accountability in the choices you make during your lifetime.

THE MAN IN THE GLASS

When you get what you want in your struggle for self
And the world makes you ruler for a day,
Just go to a mirror and look at yourself
And see what the face there has to say.

For it isn't your parents or husband or wife
Whose judgment upon you must pass,
The person whose verdict counts most in your life
Is the one staring back from the glass.

Some people might think you're a straight-shootin' chum
And call you a great gal or guy;
But the face in the glass says you're only a bum
If you can't look it straight in the eye.

That face is the face to please, never mind all the rest
For its with you clear to the end
And you've passed your most dangerous test
If the face in the glass is your friend.

You may fool the whole world down the pathway of years
And get pats on the back as you pass
But your final reward will be heartache and tears
If you've cheated the face in the glass.

What is important to you? What do you stand for? What is the most important thing in your life? Are you falling in love with the future you are planning now? Do you have answers to each of those questions? Without them you can't possibly grow, mature, and accomplish positive change using self-discipline. Finding meaning in life, growing yourself day after day, requires going out into life and living and learning new things.

Choice and change come from focused intentionality. Intention disengages automatic pilot and forces conscious choice instead of default choices made out of old programming.

Create change out of three universal environments:

- ❖ Outer Environment—The world
- ❖ Inner Environment—The self (self-concept, beliefs, values, and character)
- ❖ Interpersonal Environment—Others (family, friends, co-workers, neighbors, sales and service people, and the general public)

Here are the seven steps to successful change:

Lead Your Life Rather Than Follow Others—Choose your actions based on some goal, wish, desire, outcome that is important to you.

Focus on What You Want—You are the master gardener of your life. Your focus is your vision of how you want it to bloom. You may only have planted tulips and lilies, yet you can see the azaleas and dahlias that one day will bloom in your garden.

Do the Important Things First—When you take charge of your life and focus on what you want, you get a good instinct about what you need to be doing at any given moment. That doesn't mean that small tasks and demanding people won't try and make you believe they are more important. Use these questions: *If I stop and take care of that, what won't get done that is important? Is it worth it?*

Be All-Centered Instead of Self-Centered—Whenever your choices for change affect others, include those effects into your decision-making.

Think Baby Steps Instead of Giant Steps—Choosing to lose five pounds a month makes more sense than pushing yourself to lose twenty-five pounds in a month. You may indeed lose more than five pounds with discipline, however, success in losing twenty-five pounds pushes the envelope and stresses your body.

Fake It Until You Make It—*Act as if* is a concept that can make or break your success. You can't become something you don't know how to be. Think of a retired couple who buy a small farm.

Unless they can learn to act as if they are already farmers, their farm will fail. Ways of being are mindsets. Farmers get up early, know animal psychology, and understand the ways of land and nature more intimately than those in other professions.

Keep On Keeping On—Be resilient when you lose ground. You'll fall back into old ways. Pick yourself up, dust yourself off, put one foot in front of the other, and go deliberately forward toward your vision of what you want.

Without goals, you are like a gardener who cares for whatever comes up, rather than planting blooms and plants of choice. Your goals are personal, individual to you. You are always the goalkeeper charged with reviewing long-term goals for sense. When you periodically re-evaluate your goals, you can uncover the hidden problems that infest your success. Otherwise, you can find yourself right back into your fat clothes, off your exercise program, smoking, drinking, like the change never happened.

When you want to get thinner, most of the time, the problem comes from failing to develop the mindset of a thin person or a fit person. You haven't forced yourself to behave differently than you feel. That initial force I call *Fake it until you make it.* All it takes for success is enough practice to feel comfortable. I joined Toastmasters International when I decided I wanted to speak for a living. One young boy of eighteen stays burned in my memory. His first five-minute speech his hands and body literally shook embarrassingly, sweat dripped down from his temples, his voice fluttered, and his face flushed all the way back to his ears. I had never seen anyone that uncomfortable before an audience. Speech after speech his nervousness lessened ever so slowly. Three years later he was elected president of our chapter. Speaking before a group remained a challenge for him. Still, he finds his courage speech after speech, just like newly thin people find their courage one *no thank you* at a time.

That Toastmaster took responsibility for his goal, to learn to speak publicly. He didn't dismiss his goal by saying, *Look some people are good at standing up speaking before an audience. I'm not. It's not my fault.* He didn't say, *I know it's my own fault that I am terrible in front of an audience. But there isn't anything I can do about it.*

What the Toastmaster did I call Self-Discipline. There are two aspects of self-discipline. One reflects the first step, *Lead rather than follow others.* The other, more complex, requires you to safeguard your lead from those who would take it away from you. You have a right to yourself, your time, and your things. When you take charge of these, the rest usually falls into place.

Safeguard yourself against those who would usurp your master of your own universe status. This concept I call Setting Limits and Boundaries, a process designed to unclutter your life physically, mentally, environmentally. Clutter oppresses, suffocates, and stresses you every time you encounter it. Weed out requests from people who give you no peace. Stop taking calls you don't want to answer. Stop talking with sales people when you don't want to buy. Stop saying *yes* when you really want to say *no.*

Three types of people oppress: PESSIMISTS, ABUSERS, and THE IRRESPONSIBLE. These oppressors represent physical clutter, along with poor eating habits, lack of exercise, and neglectful body care. People oppress, most times, by taking advantage of your good nature. The atmosphere around them feels heavy, speaking to the expression, *You could cut the tension with a knife.* They drag you down, push you down, and pull down your personal productivity, as long as you let them. Obviously, resisting oppressors becomes harder when they stay in your face day in and day out. I said harder, remember, not impossible.

Mental clutter comes from overloading your mind with the unnecessary, like information, worrying about what isn't finished, gossiping, problems you don't own, and efforts to change others and the world at large. The mind's no different than any other field. You plant too much stuff in it and nothing worthwhile grows. Examine what runs through your mind. See how much is mental static and how much is information you need and use.

Emotional clutter comes from what isn't, what never was, what can't be, what isn't possible, and envy over what others enjoy. When you set your mind to making yourself an emotional mess, you can create endless possibilities. You can worry about things that relate to you. If that isn't enough you can worry about things that relate to others, expanding from your own corner of the world to the entire planet. Moving forward, when worrying about yourself and others isn't enough, you can then focus on whales, owls, the loss of popularity of the scare crow, and whether or not you are in danger of alien kidnap.

Now, I'm not saying ignore problems, but I am saying manage problems. I am saying make sure the problems are yours. You waste your time working at changing others. You can't change for them. You can only change yourself. And in setting limits and boundaries, refusing to get sucked into others' problems, you send messages to others that can result in positive change for them. Still, they made the ultimate decision to change. For example, your nineteen-year-old's hanging around the house because college isn't desirable and no jobs appeal. Your choice to stop feeding your teenager pocket money may result in a positive change. As long as you feed spending money, you enable the irresponsible behavior.

Beyond problem-solving philosophy, here's something that has worked for me for years. Time was when something went wrong, I cluttered my mind with it. *Why did that happen? What could I have done to prevent it? Will it happen again? What should I do about it?* On and on. Obviously, not much work got done when the problem greedily took over my thinking. My mother planted the seed to this solution. Put your problems away until you have time to solve them, almost like saying, *You can't play with your problems until you get your work done*. From that seed this concept evolved: Visualize putting your problems in a box, sealing it, and locking it in your closet until you finish your day's necessary work. Here's the best part. Then, you visualize taking it out and unwrapping it, IF YOU LIKE. Work with this concept and see how many times you actually forget to unwrap your problem at the end of the day.

Look, problems are always going to be there. Gilda Radner's book, *It's Always Something,* speaks to that. Self-discipline teaches you a concept, Time Quickening, choosing the best use of your time on purpose. Time quickening is the antidote to burnout. It is focused concentration compared to distracted drudgery. You focus your full boat of attention on your task. (Sorry triple-trackers, your quality can't measure up to a focused single-tracker.) Blow away any distractions, physical, mental, and environmental. Give yourself time mandates to stick to the task. Work the task according to a goal you choose to achieve, so you know the next task for the next block of time. Throw consistent blocks of time at the task until it is completed.

Distractions are physical as well as mental. There are two kinds, your body and your environment. For example, the harder my project, the hungrier I get. The other pertains to your physical environment. When you have a place for everything and keep everything in its place, you will be amazed how much time you will save. Order speaks to the physicality of remembering. Discipline makes life easier not harder. Discipline represents a plan of action, a respect for your time.

Lots of ink tells us to learn how to say no to others. With self-discipline I say give more than equal time to saying no to you. Here's an example. While waiting in line at the bank to cash a check, somebody really annoyed me. I was admittedly in a hurry, and the women ahead of me just kept chatting and chatting. Finally, I said (of course I thought politely), "Excuse me, I'd like to take my turn." The woman first glared at me, then said to the teller, "Oh, hurry, better wait on Miss 'thinks she's a really important customer.'" I didn't think I deserved that. Days later, I'm still going over and over it, reliving it, holding on to the negative emotion, even though the stimulus for the emotion was long gone. This comes from a time-consuming habit I call Demand for the Best Quality Service Every Time. Within the framework of bad habits are good habits turned inside out, can you see how a perfectly normal expectation of good service gets out of control? Good quality service means the bank is open, staffed, and I can transact my business within a reasonable amount of time. Did the chatting move my experience out of good service? No. Did the chatting move my experience out of the best quality service? In my mind it did, and I intruded negatively on three people's day directly, the chatter, the teller, and myself. The best use of my time in that situation would have been active behavior modification. Make a conscious choice instead of going on automatic from my belief that I deserve the highest quality service every time out. That belief is unrealistic, impossible, and downright disabling.

Change required me to choose my battles and say no to myself about demanding the highest quality service on each transaction. I decided to stop my war with the seller world. Do I always get it right? I don't honestly, but at least I have a positive goal to choose before I dig myself into a time-sucking war that gives poor value for my time. Remember the bad printing job?

Self-discipline/behavior modification, whatever you choose to call managing yourself, gives great benefits:

- You work smarter
- Goals are achieved faster
- Your life has more balance
- Procrastination is controlled
- Life-draining habits are reduced
- You enjoy your life more

Self-awareness is rarely enough to generate progress. Merely knowing what to do doesn't guarantee getting it done. Positive progress comes from sustained effort and self-discipline. Ask any farmer, dancer, musician, or sexy senior citizen.

When I have a problem engaging my self-discipline, I make an attitude adjustment. This computer, less than a week old, came defective and I am waiting for replacement equipment. The docking station connections are unreliable, for example, and when I plug in my laptop it takes three or more tries and my keyboard can go dead. In addition, the docking station buzzes. An attitude adjustment says, Poor people in Third World countries don't have these problems. The little children who can eat, drink, learn, and get medical care for 75 cents a day don't have these problems. All things are relative. I use this to minimize my problem and, honestly, until I started writing this, I hadn't heard the buzz for a couple of hours.

Here's another attitude adjustment I use to enhance time quickening. Say, I'm in the middle of a really busy day, lots of deadlines, things going on. I start to feel pressured. My mental alertness starts to succumb to choking. I learned this trick from Mechi Garza, a Native American elder and medicine woman, who also teaches at the International Women's Writing Guild's Skidmore College summer conference. Place both palms up toward the Great Spirit in the sky. Visualize rushing white water, smashing against rocks, coursing along. See it carrying leaves and fish. Next, turn both hands over so palms face Mother Earth. Visualize the water slowing down, gently caressing the rocks until the leaves rest atop the still water. You have just completed Mechi's Slow Down Time exercise. It also works in reverse to quicken time.

Change and self-discipline need to have a universal reach that spreads over body, mind, and spirit. Otherwise, your life is out of balance. In some ways, human bodies function like machinery. You replace worn tires on a tractor that has an old battery, old oil, and worn parts. New tires just aren't going to make much of a difference in the overall efficiency of the tractor unless you tend to the needs of its other worn parts.

Now that you have worked through growing yourself, we move on to Live and Let Live, growing good relationships with others.

Here is your Harvest Summary for Chapter 3: Self is Seed for the Life You Lead

Chapter 4

Live and Let Live

INTRODUCTION

On average, people spend 75 percent of their time speaking or listening. Obviously, communication skill building is vital in maintaining workable relationships. Yet, the great majority rarely work on listening, speaking, or communication skills. In addition, the elders in our society and Baby Boomers rarely learned listening skills, even when they went through college and graduate school.

Our purpose within this chapter is to help you attain the skills necessary to practice loving empathy as your listening goal. While a full course in effective listening is beyond the scope of this book, I believe those who chose this self-improvement book have spent enough time learning listening skills to shorten their bridges to empathic communication competency. Within this chapter, you'll learn about empathy, body language, and communication in relationships.

Likely, you already know those in emotional struggles need to trust those they confide in, and trust requires risk. For those who offer a willing ear and a gentle heart, reaching out is risky for them as well. After you've listened, people may feel comfortable enough to ask you to do more. It may be a stretch for you to move beyond listening. Someone sent me this piece on relationship risks during my struggle to help me overcome a painful breakup.

RISKS

To laugh is to risk appearing the fool.
To weep is to risk appearing sentimental.
To reach out for another is to risk involvement.
To expose feelings is to risk exposing your true self.
To place your ideas, your dreams, before a crowd is
to risk their loss.
To love is to risk not being loved in return.
To live is to risk dying.
To hope is to risk despair.
To try is to risk failure.
But risks must be taken, because the greatest hazard
in life is to risk nothing.
The person who risks nothing, does nothing, has
nothing and is nothing.
They may avoid suffering and sorrow, but they cannot
learn, feel change, grow, love, live.
Chained by their certitudes they are a slave, they have
forfeited their freedom.
Only a person who risks is free.

There are other natural barriers to empathic listening. Consider, nearly 75 percent of the population describe themselves as shy. Most people find it hard to share their troubles and feel uncomfortable listening to others' troubles. That means for most people initiating communication takes courage, because they feel afraid. Here are seven common communication fears:

- Disapproval
- Appearing foolish
- Ridicule
- Embarrassment
- Rejection
- Commitment
- Getting taken advantage of

People hold onto these fears because, all too often, these fears come true for them over and over. Recall the Johari Window mentioned earlier. One half of us lies in the shadow of mystery and only the outside half is even possible to see. When people wear false personality masks, they put even more outside of others' knowing.

You fool yourself when you believe understanding others is easy. Yet, understanding others better is always possible when you follow some do's and don'ts:

- Do make a firm commitment to work at understanding others.
- Do work at accepting others' ways, habits, likes, dislikes, strengths and weaknesses.
- Don't arrogantly assume what you aren't told, thinking you know someone inside out.
- Don't give people advice unless they specifically ask for it.

In trying to follow my own advice I developed a concept to help called The Clock of Connection.

Top Priority at 12 O'Clock – Understand Self

Next Priority at 3 O'Clock – Reduce Emotional Stress and Increase Self Love

Next Priority at 6 O'Clock – Understand Others

Final Priority at 9 O'Clock – Reduce Conflict and Increase Harmony

In the words of St. Bernard of Clairvaux: *If you wish to see, listen.*

Here are some struggles many encounter when they try to listen empathically:

- ❖ Wanting to talk when they need to be listening
- ❖ Believing they are good listeners naturally and don't have to work at listening empathically
- ❖ Scattering their focus by judging others' communication skills negatively instead of concentrating on effective listening
- ❖ Assuming and presuming instead of asking others to tell them what they are thinking, feeling, and know
- ❖ Becoming impatient when people hesitate or go on about something that is bothering them

One of the most recurring problems in communication happens when people believe others should or naturally see things the way they do. Several times, I've seen and heard Loren Eisley's story, *The Starfish Thrower,* as an illustration. The story speaks about both empathy and understanding. Here's my short version:

> A sea-worn old man walked along the beach after a storm. Helpless, hopeless starfish dotted the beach, doomed to bake to their death from the hot sun.
>
> Several feet down the beach the man spotted a young boy walking slowly picking up one starfish after another and throwing them back into the life-giving sea.
>
> The old man called out to the boy, "Son, you're wasting your time. You'll never be able to save all the starfish. What difference can the few starfish you save possibly make?"
>
> The boy called back as he threw another starfish, "It makes a lot of difference to this one."

I'll never forget the first time I recognized my ability to watch the consequences of my behavior as it happened and change the outcome. Across from me sat a young manicurist, her hands shaking as she tried to repair five out of ten recently applied nails that had broken. I didn't have time out of my hectic day to invest more time on nails I'd just applied.

After the manicurist told me, "I'm good at what I do. You expect too much and should either stop wearing nails or go someplace else," I moved from frustrated to furious. Priding myself on containing my temper (not screaming), I said, "I'm sitting here three days into new nails with half of them broken and you tell me you are good at what you do and I expect too much?"

That's when I first noticed her hands shaking. My fury cooled quickly. I had no right to create that much stress to a human being over something as unimportant as nails.

My whole tactic changed. I hated bullies and didn't like feeling like one. I said, "Look, neither of us wanted this to happen and neither of us has the extra time to deal with it."

Her hands stopped shaking and she said, "I don't mind. I like what I do. Look, I've had a horrible week. My six-year-old son exposed himself in school, and they are acting like it's all my fault. I've been fighting with my boyfriend trying to get my car back. I'm sorry I acted like I didn't care about keeping you as a customer, because I want you as my customer as long as you want to come."

Her son's school had critically questioned her abilities as a mother. She and her boyfriend were fighting. On top of that I had critically questioned her career competency. This struggling single mother had attacks in the three areas where she worked hardest to excel. She mustered every ounce of self-confidence she had left when she told me she was good at what she did. She knew at some level if she lost this battle, she'd lost it all.

At that moment three discoveries changed me forever. One unearthed the skill of on-the-spot analysis of my behavior. The second taught me that I could not only catch myself behaving badly, I could also choose immediately to change that bad behavior. Third, I watched the concept of fusing body, mind, and spirit into one essence and operating as a unit become real for me. Powerful stuff, empowering abilities. Even though my body pulsed with anger and my mind pushed my worst side to the front, my spirit could crash through with empathy. Barbara Garro finally had gotten herself together as a unified, awake, aware empathic team. I saw what was possible. After years of working at living in the present moment, I had my breakthrough, a hole in one. In-the-moment-self-awareness finally happened for me while angry emotions surged within me. My body, mind, shadow self, superior self, and spirit came together as one loving being. *Right makes might* took on a beautiful new meaning. The strength for me moved from being right to doing right.

That doesn't mean it's automatic, easy, or always possible. The same farmer grows great crops and poor crops, however, a poor farmer rarely puts forth the effort to grow great crops.

After the initial *aha* moment, doubt dampened my fragile confidence. Like an animal whose master has died, I waited, not knowing my life was forever changed. I needed confirmation that I had had an epiphany instead of a profound accident. Two seasons passed before it came.

My business planning for 1997 included replacing an obsolete fax, copier, printer, and computer. What luck, a mail order office supplier wanted my business back badly enough to send me a super sale flier that included an extra 25 percent off. I couldn't believe the timing. In the flier were the perfect fax and copier replacements, both on sale for half price, a $1,000 savings. Then I would save $250 on top of that.

Nobody's fool, I called and checked out the super sale price with the local chain office supply house. Well, the mail order house's super sale price was more than regular price at the local store.

Still, the 25 percent represented a $250 savings. Unfortunately, disappointment awaited. When I called the company, the order taker said the 25 percent didn't apply to the machines. I asked to speak with a supervisor. I told him that the copier was shown on the same page that offered the 25 percent off and that the flier said the 25 percent applied to everything in the flier. Then I went off on a rip, his company's super sale price was more than the regular price at the local office supply house. I blasted his company's misleading and fraudulent advertising methods, cited Truth in Advertising Laws, and threatened exposure.

Thirty minutes of self-righteous debate and the supervisor caved and agreed to write my order with the additional 25 percent discount. The win felt real good.

What made me take one final look at the flier, I'll never know. When I did, I saw in the tiniest print the words *Machines excluded.* My heart sunk. "I can't do this," I told him. "I just saw the tiny print that says 'machines excluded.' I can't believe I didn't see it before. It isn't right for me to take the discount now."

"I can believe you didn't see it," he said. "Most people would have taken the deal and run, but it makes me feel good that you care about being honest. I'd have done the same thing. Look, I'll give you the best deal I can. How about if I knock off the shipping and give you the machines at our cost?"

After we made the deal, I discovered that he and I shared the same belief system that nothing good comes from getting something that costs somebody else. He went on to tell me he and his family live in a Midwest town called Zion where all the streets are named after places in the Bible. I sent his family an angel story tape from my former television show, *God's Neighborhood.*

Seek out the goodness, beauty, and truth in others. Explore with me some paths leading toward understanding others and build terrific relationships.

Leo F. Buscaglia said, "It's not enough to have lived. We should be determined to live for something." May I suggest that it be creating joy for others, sharing what we have for the betterment of personkind, bringing hope to the lost and love to the lonely.

EMPATHY, RIGHT NURTURING

In *The Primal Vision,* John W. Taylor said: "Our first task in approaching another . . . [person], another culture, another religion, is to take off our shoes, for the place is holy. Else we find ourselves treading on people's dreams. More serious still we may forget that God was there before our arrival."

My oldest and best friends, one He and two She's, really accept me, virtues and vices. I trust them completely and feel comfortable telling them anything. They never judge when I discuss my problems, rather give loving empathy. Each has seen my need at times and selflessly, literally put their lives on hold to help me through something. Having them in my life has been a tremendous comfort to me. I lost one, Mae, in May 1998. How I miss her, my sensitive, brilliant sounding board, coach, confidant. Because of Mae I now use my birth name instead of the name of a man I divorced. Every time I write my name I'm grateful to Mae. For nearly thirty years, Mae was a phone call away.

True empathic communication is a mirror rather than your interpretation and judgmental feedback, all about the other person and

nothing about you. Empathy takes your feet out of your shoes and slips them into the shoes of another for the time you give to comfort them, celebrate their triumphs and enjoy birthdays, anniversaries, support them, and brainstorm about their ideas and problems.

Most people think of empathy in connection with sadness, pain, and trouble. Yet, empathic listening has universal applications in joyful times as well. Without empathy, people can dampen others' joys. A teen tells her friend about her new prom dress, all excited. Her friend asks, "Is it a designer dress?" Whoosh goes the air out of her bubble. You tell your sibling you feel good because you just got your first raise. Your sibling says, "Oh, that's nothing, I get a raise and bonus every year. You've got a long way to go before you get into my league, little brother."

As best I can, I'll describe the loving empathy I said is the most wonderful gift you can ever give anyone. Here are some of the skills and attitudes you need to put into place before you can offer others empathy:

Self-Understanding—Without the ability to understand yourself and deal with your own emotions, you are unable to understand and deal with others' emotions. (More Chapter 3)

The Support System Exercise

Think of a time when someone was really there for you, empathically understanding, offering you the strength when you felt weak from mental, emotional, or physical pain. Describe as best you can what they gave you. See if you can put their gifts into action words, such as "they comforted, listened."

Next, think of a time when you were really there for someone. Describe the time, including why you chose to put your life on hold to help someone else. What were you feeling at the time? Describe in action words what you did for the other person. If other times come to you, describe them as well.

Other Understanding—Focus, emphasis on mutual benefit, commitment, empathic listening, and really hearing and feeling for another person are some of the things that tell them you are working hard at understanding them from their point of view instead of yours.

Solid Listening Skills—Good listening requires you to stop yourself from getting in the way of another's message with your own opinions, feelings, judgments, beliefs, and way of doing things.

Unconditional Love—If you choose to offer others loving empathy, you need to work at unconditional love, one of the hardest virtues to acquire. Unconditional love says, *I always love you no matter what, but I don't always like all the things you do.* My mother had an expression she used when she felt I'd misbehaved, *I love you but I don't like you right now.*

Focused Attention—If you can't give someone all your attention during communication, postpone the communication until you can. When farmers weed young plants they focus total attention on the task because mistakes can get costly. Without 100 percent attention, listening mistakes can get costly as well, sometimes leading to misunderstandings that ruin long-standing relationships, family ties, and marriages.

It's reality check time. Within this book, it isn't possible to fully communicate an exhaustive subject such as loving empathy. Empathy is a complex subject. Several books have already been written. Here, a working knowledge discussion and general skill building are the goals driving this section.

Adapting 19th century Italian economist Vilfredo Pareto's 80-20 Principle (20 percent of best efforts produce 80 percent of the value from all your efforts), concentrate on the most important 20 percent of your communication: empathic listening. Pareto's Principle would have you communicating smarter, not harder. When you listen empathically, you get the lion's share of your information from others.

Once people realize you really care to hear them out, they are mostly happy to tell you what you need to know. It's when you cut them off mid-sentence, butt in, interrupt, assume, presume, finish their sentences, and blatantly overtalk that they close down their information pipeline to you.

There are two secrets to receiving good communication: first, be still, and second, listen. There are two secrets used by the greatest communicators: first, love; and second, empathy.

Love and empathy move your center of communication from self-awareness to global awareness where you go beyond self-interest to general interests. Only from the perspective of global awareness is empathy possible.

Here is a comparison between empathic communication and self-centered communication:

Empathic	**Self-Centered**
Speaks little	Talks too much
Listens patiently with interest	Jumps in with advice
Signals efforts to understand	Pretends to understand
Honors person's feelings	Says feelings are wrong
Hears person out	Interrupts, gets impatient
Concentrates on other person	Can hardly wait to talk
Gives support	*That's life, stop your whining*
Accepts others as they are	Makes judgments, criticizes

One of the most comforting uses of empathy is to soothe troubled hearts. And all of us suffer troubled hearts during our lifetimes. So often in an effort to stop the hurting, the well-meaning attempt to minimize it, put time frames around it, and, when all else fails, criticize the person for holding on to the hurt. When you read these in print, they seem so cold, you can hardly believe anyone would do that to another person. Yet people do it all the time.

Empathy is loving, kind, considerate, curious, supportive, gentle, quiet, patient, nurturing, warm, and feeling. People who hurt can't process your words of advice, personal stories or problem analysis. Remember, if you keep nothing else in this whole section, much of your unasked for advice gets received as judgment and criticism. The hurt can't hear your outpouring of words that attempt to drown out their sorrow. My friend Mae saw a future for me, while I could only suffer in the present. Nowhere in my abilities at that time existed the cognition to process needs in my future. She waited until just the right time when I was preparing my divorce document to suggest, "You might want to consider taking back your birth name."

In speaking as you offer empathy, comfort to another, do so in soft tones as you acknowledge their feelings from their perspective. Ask only necessary questions to clarify, confirm, help them share more. Offer help only if you really are able to do more than listen empathically. If they accept your help, ask them what you can do to help. Again, avoid telling them what you would like to do.

Empathy, a simple concept of selfless unconditional love and acceptance, difficult to accomplish, is a saving grace for troubled hearts. Practice the concept and build your skills. You'll love yourself for the good you can do when you offer empathic support to others. You truly make a difference in someone's life every single time you offer them your priceless gift of loving empathy.

Body Language, Ripe Intention

Nearly twenty years ago, I met an old man who told me he could tell me all about myself by reading my face. His system fascinated me, and started me on a long journey to understand the wordless messages people send.

Nonverbal communication has several names, kinesics, body language, and the concept goes back to Charles Darwin's *Origin of the Species*. Darwin defined the expression of emotions in man and animals. When you love a pet you and your pet learn to understand each other solely through nonverbal communication. When you think about all the things your pet has taught you about it, you see the tremendous value in working on your skill in interpreting human nonverbal communication. Recognize that a full 93 percent of your feelings and attitudes are communicated with tone of voice and nonverbal signaling and positioning.

The two languages human babies learn are nonverbal. The first, visual, relates to three-dimensional pictures where babies see colors, bright lights, shadows, and shapes. The second, body language, relates to the cues babies take from caregivers and the cues they learn to give to caregivers.

Like babies, the best interpreters of body language are those who approach nonverbal language within a context instead of relying on one gesture. Nonverbal communication occurs within a matrix that includes facial expressions, body movements, spatial cues, verbalization, and a situation. A single gesture within this broad spectrum rarely tells the complete nonverbal message. All body language is situational. Lazy broad-brush interpretations can spoil communications. Facial expressions can be faked. For example, a true smile is quick, involves the top of the face including the eyes. The phony

The Me I See Exercise

Find a hand mirror, the bigger the better. Go to a large mirror where the light is especially good. You will be looking for differences in the left and right sides of your face. Folklore says that the left side of your face comes from your mother and the right side of your face comes from your father. They say the more differences there are in the two halves of your face, the greater the difference in the looks of your parents.

Look at your face as a painter would. Begin with your eyebrows. Are they even, or is one significantly higher or lower than the other? My left eyebrow, for example, is much higher than the right. Now, look at your eyes. Is one larger or smaller than the other? Again, my left eye is a wee bit larger than my right eye. How about your nose? Is it longer or shorter on one side? How about larger on one side than the other? Again, my left nostril is bigger than my right. How about your mouth? One side of your lips thinner or thicker than the other? One side of your mouth higher than the other? I found my mouth to be slightly crooked.

Now, check out your findings in the hand mirror. Position the hand mirror so that you can look into the mirror and see your face in the big mirror. Look at your face full view, then left side and right side, left profile, and right profile. When I do this, my mouth looks much more crooked and my eyes look much more mismatched. Now, can you see why movie stars always want the camera on their good side?

Are you wondering why this exercise? The purpose is to show you how to catch subtle differences in facial features that can indicate feelings, thoughts, reactions. So, you do exercises to practice on your own face, the face that you rarely see in conversations. Have some fun with this exercise. Get to know your face. Show yourself

smile lasts longer and involves only the bottom of the face. The well-interpreted crossed-arm gesture can certainly mean rejection, but can also be a favorite stance of large-breasted women, defensiveness, feeling cold, or, stretching a bit, self-hugging. A little knowledge about nonverbal communication can lead to more confusion than enlightenment. Like listening and speaking, skill in nonverbal interpretation requires a learned adeptness in concurrent multi-faceted activities.

People's bodies tend to be much more truthful than their words. Every move made with the body makes the subject of interpretation. The face and hands reveal the most secrets to those who know how to read them. Here are some of the categories behavioral scientists recognize regarding nonverbal gestures:

Comfort: relaxed body and facial muscles, flexible limbs

Nervous: busy hands, throat clearing, shallow breathing, blushing

Interested: leaning forward, alert facial expressions

Suspicious: look or move away, side glance, button up, lift eyebrow

Boredom: tap fingers or feet, click pen, jiggle change, doodle

Rejection: cross arms, rub nose, ear or eyes, turn back, scowl

Cooperation: smile, positioned in listening posture

Confidence: eye contact, pyramid hands, feet up

Tension: tight jaw, stiff upper lip, hard eyes

Openness: open jacket, open hands, smile

Defensiveness: reversed chair, fist, finger pointing

Acceptance-Seeking:clench hands, bite on things

Frustration: shallow breaths, rub back of neck, roll eyes

Evaluating: tilt head, stroke chin, walk around

Body language tells you how you are doing in your communications much faster than words. If someone believes what you say, they tend to react immediately with eye contact. How can you tell if someone is lying? Look for subtle cues, because accomplished liars know several body language tricks. The whole story of the most famous liar, *Pinocchio,* centers around the nose revealing when someone is lying. No single gesture, however, can accurately predict lying. In real life, the pupils of the

some smiles, little ones, surprised ones, small, subtle ones, curious ones, questioning ones. Frown. Look disappointed, sad, disgusted, annoyed, angry, happy, worried, afraid, puzzled. Show yourself all the faces you've shown everyone you know all your life. Many of my students find this a fascinating exercise. Others approach it reluctantly, and then tell me they really got caught up in it. Whatever your initial thought, I hope you'll humor me and really do the exercise. Learning the faces you show to the world is good information. I promise you, you'll want to change at least one or two of them.

eyes tend to grow larger and lids flutter. Amateur liars often raise their voices. Knowing these tell-tale signs, accomplished liars lower their voices and eyes. Look for signs of discomfort, anxious looks, tension, lip biting, face touching, phony smile, and feet shifting. Liars' expressions often give away their words as lies. They frown when the words are friendly, smile when their words are serious, and cover their mouths while speaking.

Obviously, the entire spectrum of nonverbal communication can only be covered as the single subject of a whole book. Within this chapter, I intend to increase your awareness of what others' bodies tell you while they are verbally communicating with you. And also to help you also recognize that your body language speaks volumes to others as well. So, first body language is a two-fold flow that includes not only what we read in others but also what we send out when we communicate. You need to pay as much attention to your nonverbal signals as you do to others if you really want to be on top of what's going on in your communication.

Here's my Stoplight Technique to help you do that:

- Red signifying Communication Conflicts;
- Yellow indicating Communication Change; and
- Green meaning Cooperative Communication.

Red signals tell you something is obviously wrong. Flaming red has a set face, clenched hands, folded arms looking back at you. Not so obvious red signals include various types of nose touching that indicate the listener is suspicious of what you are saying. At red, you need to get your listener back. Soften your voice, slow down your rate of speech, ask some questions, and clarify.

Yellow signals are conflicting, showing a move to red or to green. You may see a relaxed face but a clenched fist or crossed legs. Attention may be inconsistent. The person may move away from you. Follow the suggestions during red signals to move the person to the receptive green signal.

Green signals are your goal signals. In green your listener is obviously receptive, interested, relaxed, giving you positive feedback. The communication is productive.

Body language also incorporates the six senses. Yes, all the senses. Sight, hearing, taste, smell, touch, and intuition come into play during nonverbal communication. Think about how many times you have heard the expression, *I can feel the tension in this room.* More and more people are using their sixth sense, the sense that tells you something is up with another person. I've had my intuition rout out secrets, surprises, excitement, good news, bad news, discoveries, and new skills.

Nonverbal communication moves beyond merely watching, which the blind cannot do, and listening for tone changes and hesitation, which the deaf cannot do. Like Neurolinguistic Programming, sensual nonverbal communication raises receivers' levels of comprehension. If you think smell and taste push the body language envelope, learn from the words of Helen Keller, an amazing philosopher who could neither see nor hear, "In the odor of young men there is something elemental as of fire, storm, and salt sea. It pulsates with buoyancy and desire."

Here's how body language helps me understand others. Eyes tell me whether or not someone new likes me. Facial expressions tell me whether or not someone wants to keep talking with me. Standing and sitting stances tell me whether people are excited, interested, bored, or impatient with interactions with me. When people roll their eyes north, south, east or west, I know they are thinking. Lack of eye contact tells me people are shy, evasive or extremely uncomfortable with one-on-one communication.

Here's an example. Once while attending a Claudio Naranjo advanced personal growth Enneagram workshop, someone piqued my interest and I went up and introduced myself to her. She literally pulled herself into herself, with her face looking anxious, her voice tenuous. She made it clear that I had invaded her space and she did not like it one bit. Later on in the seminar, I gathered up my investigator courage and approached her again. This time, I kept my physical distance, spoke purposely more softly and slowly, and most important, asked her permission to ask her a question. This time she was visibly more relaxed and receptive. I mentioned that I felt I made her uncomfortable the last time I approached her and I wished to check with her that my impression was correct. She said it was. For her, my energy felt too intense. She felt invaded. She just wanted to get away from me. My aggressive Type A personality crashed against her laid-back Type B personality. We had an instructive conversation, but I never made the connection I had hoped to make.

Freud said, "No mortal can keep a secret. If . . . lips are silent, . . . [one] chatters with fingertips; betrayal oozes out of . . . [one] at every pore."

As a general rule, body language from 68 facial features and over 100 behavioral traits comprise 60-90 percent of the messages people convey. There are some 200 muscles in the face. From the skull, you think, process information, analyze, make judgments, reach conclusions, and step-by-step decide to act. All the while, your head and facial muscles reflect what's going on inside:

The Head—No matter what you say verbally, whichever way you nod your head when you say it is more true than your words.

Above the Eyes—You show spontaneous reactions as you wrinkle the forehead up in surprise and downward when confused.

The Eyes—These emotion windows tell what you feel, show your comfort in situations, fear, like, dislike, joy, sorrow, happiness, confusion, suspicion, and anger.

The Nose—Touch the nose and that indicates uncertainty, could be lying, could be suspicion. Flare the nostrils and that indicates frustration.

The Mouth—Out of the 50 different smiles, psychologist Paul Ekman of the University of California School of Medicine, says only about 18 are authentic (*Telling Lies,* Paul Eckman, W.W. Norton, 1995). A smile that shows only the upper teeth can mean that a person is really uncomfortable with you. The mouth, rather than the eyes, is the most expressive part of the face. Lip biting indicates uncertainty; pursed lips indicate disagreement of some type; and index finger to lips indicates pondering.

The Jaw—Speaks to authority. Rubbing the jaw can mean pondering. Jut it out and you probably disagree. You clench it when you tense up.

Personal space issues are also important in reading nonverbal communication signals. People are territorial creatures and have a sense of personal space along with a sense of the criterion for violating it. People have favorite seats at the dinner table, in the living room or recreation room, at the theatre, in workshops, in classrooms, and in restaurants. Americans have different cultural definitions of personal space than other countries. For Americans, the general guideline is:

- ❖ Half a Foot—intimate, a very close space conducive to whispers
- ❖ One Foot—still close usually for private conversations
- ❖ One to two Feet—again soft voice indoors, but full voice outdoors
- ❖ Two to four Feet—comfortable distance when meeting new people

How do you begin training yourself to use your six senses to read nonverbal communication signals? Use the traffic signal along with the Movie-Goer Technique. Whenever you are talking, you can't hear the movie. There is no rewind, so you lose what was said. Whenever you stop listening, you lose what is going on and can globally lose what the whole movie is about. Think of the difference between black and white images and color images. Sensual communication is always in vivid color.

I conducted an experiment to discover just how much attention people were paying to my face. Onto my black eyes I placed bright blue contact lenses. Now, these are Paul Newman blue, nothing subtle about the color. I gave a presentation to a group I had been meeting with for several months. Not one noticed the eye color change. I wore my big blues to a large local business show where I knew most of the business people exhibiting. Not one noticed my eyes. What they did notice was something was different. You look great! You've lost weight haven't you? (I hadn't.) I really like you in that blue suit. Something is really different about you. Did you change your hair? Your hair looks darker; did you do something to it? (God colored my hair when He made me and I've never had the temerity to disagree with his color choice.) And so it went for two-and-a-half hours. No one has yet noticed the blue or violet eye color changes unless I specifically show them.

Read body language in your communications and you will be literally head and shoulders ahead of others in the amount of information you gather.

Communication, Thoughtful Watering

Jim Armstrong gave me this advice: *Always tell the truth, but not a harsh truth.* There are no mistakes. If there were, this universe would have ended a long time ago.

From that lesson, I developed my first Relationship Mission Statement:

> To those I choose to have relationships with, I owe the highest quality of me humanly possible. I owe them the highest possible degree of my love, my understanding, my commitment to the relationship, my willingness to listen to them, to help them, to

share with them, to accept what they offer me in the relationships, and appreciate it.

People behave themselves into communication problems. When the conflict comes, most people, contrary to popular beliefs, are not fighting to prove themselves right, but rather to feel respected, understood, and valued in the relationship.

No easy relationship exists. One statistic stated that the average couple spends 17 minutes in real conversation each week out of 10,080 minutes. You have to work hard to live under the same roof in harmony with other people. You have to work even harder if you want meaningful relationships with them. What self-awareness and other-awareness do is help you better self-manage. Yes, all the fixing up is about you, never them. You can't change them. The best you can ever do is change yourself and hope to start positive changes in others that strengthen the relationship.

I developed two problem-solving pyramids to use as guides in building relationships and fixing relationship breakdowns. Remember these one-to-five word pyramids when you want to relax strained relations with others.

Building Pyramid	**Fixing Pyramid**
1. We	1. Please
2. May I	2. I'm sorry
3. Tell me more	3. I acted badly
4. I want to understand	4. I know you are hurting
5. Let us accept we disagree	5. Help me work through this

These pyramids join those in relationships together to work on their joint project, the relationship. This gives each person a stake in something bigger than themselves. You begin to look at your actions in helping or hurting your joint project, the relationship. This gives you a common ground on which to build and forms a natural segue for you to search for ways you agree or are alike rather than give center stage to your differences. You find what you look for. When you look for common ground that's positive. When you focus on differences that's negative. Sound simplistic? You may find it is easier to read than practice in your relationships. Positive attitude communication is hard work because you constantly find yourself pushing yourself out of the way to see the other person's view, feel for the other person, and act in mutually beneficial ways.

Common Ground or Win-Win communication works because people like people who make them feel good about themselves. Pointing out common ground makes both of you feel connected, good about the relationship.

Back in the 1980s I developed a Heart to Heart communication technique to move people toward a universal concept: Love is all there is here. In teaching the concept, I found there is a misconception about the voice of the heart. The heart is much more than emotions. The heart of anything is its essence, the most important part. Within that concept, the heart is the essence of your humanness, the true spirit of who you are as an individual. At the heart level humans are much more alike than they are different. That's why all human connection occurs at the heart level.

Love fails you only if you don't, can't or won't give it. You've no doubt heard unconditional love described as the ultimate kind of love, the most loving of all types of love. The Greeks long ago named this ultimate love *agape*. Unconditional love forms the cornerstone in relationship-building. As my mother taught me long ago, always liking others in relationships is impossible, yet once loving, always loving is possible. Once loving, always loving is a gift given forever. Beyond my mother's grave I still feel her love. She's there when I see things that came from her. She rises up from my heart when something triggers memories of her. She's in my dreams. She brings on smiles when I see something she'd enjoy. I appreciate the goodness she bestowed upon me for forty years, and I love and appreciate her more every day.

The parent-child relationship I believe is the most demanding and rewarding of all relationships because you grow two lives and see two fruits, yours and your child's. Parenting I found to be an exciting roller-coaster ride that never stops being exciting. How much my daughters have taught me as they see me with loving eyes and hearts that want the best for me.

I remember the day my daughter focused loving black eyes on me and proclaimed, "I love your self-confidence." Another day, she focused her fiery black eyes on me and declared, "You're so full of yourself!" *Well, indeed, if I'm not full of myself who would be?* So, some days I work for my daughter and other days I don't. So be it. But every day I work for myself, and that is as it should be. *Blessed are the flexible, for they shall not be bent out of shape.* If I can't figure out how to take care of myself whom I know best, how could I possibly be competent to care for my family and friends. I believe the adage: *To thine own self be true.*

Hurt and anger happen in relationships. Sometimes you bite your tongue. You make a habit out of asking yourself how important is this really? You need to do what you can to move beyond episodes of hurt and anger if you want to enjoy the peace and happiness that also happens in relationships. Two keys to moving from the place of hurt and anger to the place of peace and happiness are understanding and forgiveness. The deeper the cut of the hurt, the harder the understanding and forgiveness. Forgiveness means letting go of the hurt. That's why forgiveness is said to be healing both for the forgiven and the forgiver.

Those who have the hardest time forgiving, I find, are those who tend to take things personally and those with big egos. The first type has a center of the universe complex, feeling everything is about them. They constantly defend punches never thrown. The second types are so full of themselves there is little room for anyone else. They are stuck in *I* Mode unable to move into *We* Mode.

Both of these types tend to send blaming *You* messages in their communication instead of self-responsible *I* messages. *You never do what I want* instead of *I'd like to choose the restaurant this time. I* statements are personal, specific, direct, sensitive, and relate to the present situation only.

My voice coach, Joe Balfior, reminded me often:

> Your whole body is involved in communicating, not just the top of your head or from the neck up. And all of you needs to work to reach the other person. That other person is your target. If that person is two feet away, it takes less projecting than if the person is twelve feet away. You need to think about what the other person is saying and the messages you give back. Without thinking the voice is mechanical without purpose other than noise. Without caring, you talk at people instead of to them.

Out of Balfior's teachings, I created a message model.

	General	
Head = Facts	**+**	**Heart = Feelings**
	Specific	

Intent

Integrity

Accountability

Responsibility

People come to discussions with different needs, value systems, mental and physical states. Is it any wonder people engage in so much pointless conflict? Much time gets wasted defending personal positions and attacking others. Successful communication makes an impact that initiates understanding, influences thought, and moves the people to purposeful closure of issues. Whenever you have two people in the same place for any period of time, conflict results. People's wants and needs differ. Actually, when there is no conflict in a relationship, there is likely little buy-in, commitment, or serious personal investment. Working through conflicts toward understanding and cooperation becomes a relationship-building learning curve that strengthens the bond between people.

In *Instructive Moments With the Savior*, Ken Giresaid that in demonstrating whatit mean to be a good neighbor,the Sam!ritan defined the meaning of love. *Love doesn't look away. And it doesn't walk away. It involves itself. It inconveniences itself. It indebts itself.*

When you look for a significant other love relationship, you'll have a better relationship track record when you love with your eyes open. While this initially may sound contradictory to the good neighbor quote above, it actually speaks to a different kind of relationship. A life partner relationship choice requires a clear understanding of who each partner is and how the two could build a life together. Too many relationships begin to fill self-serving needs and end when the other person runs out of the right goods. These people, or one of them, may be in need rather than in love.

I counseled one man who was totally perplexed about his marriage troubles. Less than a year after the marriage, they were living apart. *I don't understand what happened. Before we were married, everything about me was wonderful. After we moved in together nothing about me was any good.* They'd married after knowing each other less than six months. Before they married, they saw each other a few times a week, never had harsh words. He was a great kidder, gifted at put-down humor. Through the eyes of new love, he was funny in small doses. Day in and day out, his kidding became lying and his humor became *always putting me down*. She was constantly mad at him and he never knew why. He hadn't changed. Before they were married all they saw were their positive qualities. Once they lived together all they saw were their negative qualities. They had gone to workshops, been through counseling, and nothing worked. He felt hopeless. He wanted her to understand him and she wanted him to understand her.

From Peter Ustinov, *marriage is like a three-speed gearbox: affection, friendship, love*. It is not advisable to crash your gears and go right through to love straightaway. You need to ease your way through. The basis of love is respect, and that needs to be learned from affection and friendship.

When love works people grow positively within the relationship. Relationships are learning experiences. Eventually you learn that yes-people may let you down more often than no-people who come through in the end. People are full of contradictions by nature.

Here is a beginner Bare Bones Three-Step Communication Guide:

- ❖ Know what you want to happen
- ❖ Have the ability to flex
- ❖ Have the sensory experience skills to notice when you get positive responses and when you get negative responses

Sometimes you just need to turn on your sense of humor and accept that certain things are just certain ways. For example, I have learned from all my friends and relatives that I am incapable of loading their dishwashers. Now, I have a dishwasher of my own that I load all by myself. The dishes, pots, pans, glasses, and silverware all get clean. That does not matter one iota to them, let me tell you. So when I am over at their houses, I clear their tables only. Then I take my stuffed owl posture and watch them curiously as they load their dishwasher the right way.

Charles R. Swindoll, in *Growing Strong in the Seasons of Life,* said, *God, our wise and creative Maker, has been pleased to make everyone different and no one perfect. The sooner we appreciate and accept that fact, the deeper we will appreciate and accept one another, just as our Designer planned us.*

Since no two people are alike, it helps you to understand all you can about people. Otherwise you won't have a prayer in your relationships. Like anything else you choose to do well, communication requires know-how, skill maintenance, practice and commitment to enhancement. The greats in all fields keep increasing their abilities with regular and challenging practice.

When people ask me how they can become better communicators, I tell them simply *want to.* Personal desire beats out any other emotional motivator. Someone telling you you can't communicate, don't share your feelings, and don't listen rarely will move you to action.

Lack of understanding in relationships becomes a double-edged sword. When you don't understand yourself you bring confusion to all your communications. When you don't understand others, you get confused in all your communications.

Understanding others is vital to good communication, because absolute reality is nonexistent. What exists are subjective conceptions of reality. Is the sea blue, green or aquamarine? Who is looking?

Here's what happens for you when you do learn to communicate well:

- People do what you'd like them to do more often.
- You are liked more, loved more.
- People anger you less often.
- You get less frustrated in your interactions with others.
- You understand others and what they want more clearly.
- You understand others' ways and take their actions less personally.
- You have real points to get across because you are more often prepared for conversations.
- You talk less yet get your points across more clearly.
- Your ability to get things done goes way up.

How many times in shattered relationships do people lament, *I never could figure out what they wanted.* All people have emotional needs, wants and rights. Here are three basic needs:

Need for Privacy—Personal space, to be alone, to stow things, to work, to play, to rest, to relax.

Need to Feel Special—People need loving affection and assurance that they count for something that others' value, that makes people want to be with them and pay attention to them, attention that makes them proud to be who they are.

Need for Excitement—People crave surprise, challenge, risk, learning something new, stimulants that keep them from getting bored with life.

Add to those needs:

Nine Wants People Have in Relationships:

- ❖ The romantic stimulation of good chemistry
- ❖ Feel accepted for who they are and just being together
- ❖ Feel culturally compatible
- ❖ Feel proud in introducing to family and friends
- ❖ The stimulus of mutual caring
- ❖ Intellectual compatibility
- ❖ Enjoy doing things together
- ❖ Feel respected and comfortable discussing things
- ❖ Feel spiritually compatible

Finally, add:

Nine General Relationship Rights:

- ❖ Have personal freedom and independence
- ❖ Be considered in decisions that affect me
- ❖ Refuse requests without feeling guilty or selfish
- ❖ Feel and express anger

- ❖ Expect my needs and opinions carry the same weight as others
- ❖ Fight for behavior changes from others when they infringe on my rights
- ❖ Express healthy competitive drive and strive for achievement
- ❖ Set priorities for living my own life
- ❖ Strive for personal and spiritual self-actualization

When I realized that my first Relationship Mission Statement excluded my needs, I wrote a second Relationship Mission Statement:

> Every day I clearly nurture my physical, social, mental, and spiritual selves in balance.
>
> Every day, I keep my feet grounded, appreciate nature and live life with my whole self.
>
> Every day I reflect on life, do my best, be my best, love my best, give my best, and make the best choices to achieve the highest quality of life my God-given gifts allow.
>
> Every day I value my God-given free will and the free will of others and recognize the balance and the reality of interdependence.
>
> Every day I am patient with myself and others as I strive to build a legacy of my gifts to help people achieve their best selves.
>
> Every day I exercise my mind and body, feed them thoughtfully and receive from them their best.
>
> Every day I laugh, look for fun, and the light side of life.
>
> Every day I use my intuition to see the truth, to find the messages in challenges, and stay on track when strong forces of my own nature, and others, make it difficult.

> Every day I feel gratefulness for those in my life and those I meet on my path and I accept and give abundantly.

The mission is in line with Martin Buber's *I-thou* dialogue. With the I-thou, attitude you value the other person as equally important in relationships. In comparison, Buber's *I-it* communication attitude is a monologue that places little value on the needs, wants, and rights of others in a relationship. The *I-it* attitude sees others as servants to control and manipulate.

No matter how hard you work at harmonious communication, you're apt to meet people loaded for bear, ready to fight. They are going to generalize all over the place, blow things out of proportion, jump to conclusions, blame you, guilt you, and interpret negatively. Here are some things you can consciously do to avoid getting sucked into the fight they are determined to have with you:

❖ Remember one who angers you controls you.

❖ You don't have to answer people's questions or accusations.

❖ Ignore name-calling and other attempts to goad you into stupid behavior; people ridicule when they have no logical argument for their position.

❖ Never accept nameless sources to condemn your behavior.

❖ Use your sense of humor to grossly exaggerate the situation.

❖ Get away as fast as you can from conversations going nowhere.

❖ It doesn't feel good when people judge you off-handedly, fail to ever recognize their part in relationship problems, punish you with silent treatment, and dismiss your feelings as stupid.

❖ It feels worse when people try to intimidate you under a guise of sophisticated old Greek rhetoric but actually try to steam-roll you with illogical fallacies:

1. Passionate pleading may really be a phony Appeal to Emotions.
2. When someone contradicts you with majority opinion, they are demanding you jump onto the Bandwagon Fallacy.
3. Unsupported Circular Reasoning/Begging the Question assumes an unsupported conclusion—The doctor is right because the doctor is the doctor.
4. When someone tries to force you to choose between two unacceptable choices, this is the False Dilemma fallacy, because there are likely more options than you are being offered.
5. Distracting you from the important issue, someone may throw a Red Herring or weaker issue at you again and again.
6. When someone uses off-point argument to derail or weaken your position, it's called a Straw Man Argument.

Sometimes you just can't get away from the people who drive you to distraction in communication. You married them, live with them, work with them, or share their blood. So, you have to work your way through situations. Frame your communication into a Window of Understanding:

Bottom Frame—Gather information and know what you want.

Left Side—Seek to understand the other person's position.

Right Side—Give information about your position.

Top Frame—Move the solution into win-win whenever possible.

I know these little boxes, numbers, and bullets sound easy when you are reading and are not so easy when your emotions are churning and there is an emotional person facing you. Here are two comparative 10-point charts you can program into your mind to call up:

Hallmarks of Poor Communication

1. Rushed, on the run
2. Fielding distraction
3. Pushing position on others
4. Dictating actions for others to do
5. Saying others are wrong

Hallmarks of Poor Understanding

1. Closed-minded
2. Impatient listening
3. Inattentive
4. Interrupting
5. Rejecting body language

Hallmarks of Clear Communication

1. Assertive
2. Authentic
3. Focused
4. Accepting
5. Comfortable

Hallmarks of Clear Understanding

1. Openness
2. Empathic Listening
3. Objective
4. Clarify with Questions
5. Good Intentions

Sometimes people bend too far one way or the other in their communications with the best of intentions. For example, submissive people fail to realize they are being emotionally dishonest. When you give and you resent it, you can't feel good about your decision. Your decision is not your truth. Aggressive people's comments they say are honest are put-downs masquerading as truth. *The blue slacks are better; they don't make you look as fat.* Better is directness, truth without unnecessary disclosure.

Much, if not all, you'll read here directs you to manage yourself. You are never the problem. The problem is the problem. People can take you for granted, speak for you, and volunteer your services only if you let them. You can escape from button-pushing, string-pulling, and political traps.

Communication skills are learned behaviors. You suspend beliefs, assumptions, perceptions, and any other biases when you learn to be objective. When something that you don't like is happening ask yourself some questions: *What assumptions am I making? What perceptions do I hold in this situation? What lesson can I learn from this problem?*

Help people understand your position with feeling messages: *When you tell people about my mistakes, I feel stupid before them, and I feel disrespected by you. Because I am sensitive to criticism, I would like you to stop using me for laughs when we are with other people. It hurts my feelings and spoils my time. I would like you to find some other light topic to make people laugh. What do you think?*

Lots of arguments begin when someone forgets an occasion: *Why are you making such a big deal out of your birthday? Look I'm good for the present. Can't you understand I may have had some other things on my mind, like the promotion I didn't get?* Do people make too much of such forgetfulness? I remember the first and only time my father and I both forget my parents' anniversary. I came bopping in, saw flowers in the living room, and asked my mom, "What are the flowers for, Mom?" She said, "It's our anniversary. The flowers are from Aunt Dot and Uncle Joe." I looked at my father's face and said, "Don't tell me you forgot, too!" Both feet firmly planted in my mouth, I just wanted to die. My mother's placid silence pained us more than if she had beaten us with pokers. You may wonder how my father handled the situation. He apologized sincerely, and then went on with his night, knowing he couldn't fix it, and determined never to forget again. Neither my father nor I ever forgot again.

When you forget a person's occasion, you forget the whole person, not just an event. Do whatever you have to do to make sure that you remember and celebrate the occasions of those you love, like, and care about.

While it is important to choose your battles wisely, avoid thinking that good communication is about giving in, being quiet, and taking whatever the world throws at you. Good communication is about understanding and making yourself understood. My mother stood up for herself in her own way. A seed of good communications is the willingness to assert yourself in your communications. Father Dennis Murphy told this story during his homily, "Into the dark kitchen came Mama Mouse and her kittens. Following the baseboards, they smelled the scent of the stove. Then mama mouse saw the big, ugly cat. Mama Mouse pulled herself up straight and strong and roared, 'Ruff, ruff!'" The scared cat ran. The moral of the story: *If you want to get along in this world you must speak a language each person will understand.*

Remember, when you fail to react to an act of another you set a precedent that creates a right. If it happens again, you have essentially lost your right to complain.

Positive assertiveness highlights the mutual benefits in doing something the way you'd like it done, frames desires into what you do want rather than don't want, highlights areas of agreement, and seeks to be reasonable rather than right. In any negotiation, you need to look at the situation within the context of the big picture of your relationship. Always ask yourself if a battle is one you need to fight, want to fight, and must win. Even when you feel you must fight forward, go in knowing what is negotiable and what is not.

One of the consequences of living in the world is dealing with the differences between men and women. I know I've done a lot of talking about positive attitude and not getting stuck in negativity. Still, you ignore the basic differences in attitudes and behaviors of men and women to your communication peril.

Loving, intuitive, nurturing, and cooperative people create the most harmonious relationships. Cooperative people are simply more lovable both in the short and long term. They are more likely to stay turned on, tuned in, and committed to their relationships. Relationships with this type of person tend to work because their attitude creates more good times than bad. Their relationships tend to more equally distributed power, exist in the present moment, and allow each person in the relationship to make honest choices without fear of guilt, shame, or retributions. Examples of public honoring, respectful relationships include Joanne Woodward and Paul Newman, Paul and the late Linda McCartney.

Within cooperative relationships there is still freedom, but also consideration of the other person, sharing and support. It is a freedom without infringing on the freedom of the other, a freedom that doesn't threaten the other's security in the relationship. Cooperation in a partnership relationship keeps both parties in the loop of each other's lives.

Cooperative relationships with their more reliable, consistent behavior build trust, vital to long-lasting partnerships. What characteristics do long-term loving relationships share in common?

- ❖ Comfortable with each other right from the start, and share a fine friendship
- ❖ Can tell each other anything
- ❖ Share an enduring sexual attraction and love to love each other
- ❖ Accept each other for who they are, fabulous traits and foibles
- ❖ Create comfortable routines and traditions
- ❖ Freely discuss and share dreams for the future
- ❖ Are authentic and honest with each other
- ❖ Both are free to be who they are and who they grow to be
- ❖ Who's in charge is determined by who's the best qualified
- ❖ Disagreements are spoken, settled, and neither partner holds grudges

All through the above characteristics there runs a thread of trust, a knowing that their significant other person has their best interest at heart. Romantic love without trust equals heartache no matter how much one may love another. Sometimes communication misunderstandings erode trust.

Adam and Eve both work and agree to spend Saturdays together. For Adam, the Saturday thing is a go unless something important comes up. For Eve, it is a sacred promise.

One Saturday Adam told Eve he was going hunting with the guys. Eve said, "Okay Adam" rather quietly, hoping Adam would see how disappointed she was. For Adam, that was the end of the discussion. For Eve, it was a terrible thing for Adam to do to her. She had lots of Saturday invitations that she turned down so she could keep her promise to Adam. She spent most of Saturday crying and getting more and more angry.

On Sunday, Adam and Eve had a huge fight and Adam stormed out telling Eve she was not running his life and he would go hunting, fishing, or flying a kite whenever he felt like it. Eve was thoroughly confused since Adam broke his promise about their Saturdays together, and now he was mad at her.

What went wrong? Certainly, not enough discussion took place before the promise was made. From Adam's point of view he had not made a solemn promise but a general agreement. He did not buy in, probably went along to avoid an argument. Eve could have spoken up immediately when Adam said he was going hunting with an assertive, "Nice try, Adam, but we made a Saturdays together agreement. Of course, hunting could still work. I'd love to hunt for some new suits for us." By being immediately assertive, Eve would be in a much better position for discussion. If Adam were testing the waters, he would know where he stood. At least, Eve would give Adam a chance to salvage their Saturday together. By failing to speak up while Adam could reverse his decision, Eve set herself up for her miserable Saturday. By no means do I intend to diminish Adam's light attitude about his promise to Eve. The example shows Adam took charge, asserted his power, and acted out aggressively. Eve did not do any assertive things immediately. She suffered first and spoke up after fixing the problem became impossible.

Women are often so afraid of being called the B-word. Out of that fear they let men get away with things a man would never tolerate. When women have doubts about speaking up, they need to ask themselves a question, *How would he react if I acted that way toward him?*

The sixth wife of Norman Mailer, painter Norris Church, was interviewed by Sam Donaldson on *ABC's Prime Time Live*. She described her life with Mailer, . . . *like living in a zoo. He's a tiger sometimes, he's a lamb sometimes, he's a monkey on occasion, and a fair amount of time he's a jackass. . . . He's like all men, he's different every day.*

Here's what the hopeless husband in the above story said, "She's always getting mad at me. When I ask her 'what's wrong?' she says, 'You know what you did.' I don't have a clue. She won't tell me for days, weeks on end. How can we ever solve our problems if she won't tell me what they are?"

Here's this couple's version of a promise is a promise. He gets home well before 6 p.m. when she comes in. So he makes dinner. It's ready as soon as she walks in the door. She said, "I like to unwind, relax, open the mail, before I eat. I'd rather eat at 7 p.m." He said, "I like to eat at 6 p.m., so why don't we compromise and eat at 6:30 p.m.?" They agreed. One day the raviolis were ready at 6:20 p.m. and he called her into dinner. She said, "I'll be in at 6:30." He got angry. "It's not my fault the raviolis got ready early. You see if I cook for you again!" He felt unappreciated, like a fool for being so good to her. She felt pressured. Truth is she never asked him to cook for her in the first place.

Oscar Wilde said: *Men marry because they are tired [of the single life]; women marry because they are curious [about having a man of their own]. Both are disappointed [and they fight].*

The differences between men and women sure do cause some measure of trouble. Men, you see, don't talk enough and women tend to talk too much. So women have to listen really carefully to the men to get their message which is really hard when they are so busy talking. If women listen, men usually tell the truth. Men on the other hand have to mine all the talk from women to find the gem stones they need to understand. It's really hard for men to keep paying attention long enough to find the gem stones. Men have shorter attention spans than women.

Men are better at math than women and women have better memories. So men will remember how many times they fought and women will remember who was to blame for every fight.

Men tend not to take things personally and recover from attacks quickly. Men forget problems by not thinking or talking about them. Women tend to take things personally and recover from attacks slowly if at all. Women forget problems by airing them out and processing them until they can put them aside. For men conversation is for sharing information and is fact or rationality driven. For women conversation is a symbol of caring and friendship and is feelings or emotion driven.

Men are much more preoccupied with sex than women. Men often give names to their private parts. I have yet to hear of a woman who named hers. Men need more sex than intimacy and women need more intimacy than sex. There are at least 150 men's magazines and one *Playgirl.* There are 25,000 sex phone lines for men and about three for women.

Here are some important differences that can sour male-female communication:

- ❖ Women's conversations circle around topics while men converse in a straight line and someone is supposed to win.
- ❖ Men like more space and women want more closeness.
- ❖ Women give what they want in relationships while men go after what they want.
- ❖ Men fear being pushed around and women fear being pushed away.

- ❖ Women pull in their anger while men push theirs out.
- ❖ Men pick fights to push others away and women pick fights to clear the air and get closer.
- ❖ Women passively gossip and backbite when angry and men aggressively ignore and put down.
- ❖ Men tend to be self-focused and women tend to be other-focused.

Women can be more successful in communications with men by being Brief, Specific, Direct, Witty, and Ask for Important Changes in Behavior.

Men can be more successful in communications with women by being Understanding, Empathic, Respectful, and Consider the Conversation a Win only When Both of Them Win.

FROM *THE SHOES OF THE FISHERMAN:*

It costs so much to be a full human being, there are very few who have the enlightenment or courage to pay the price. One has to abandon altogether the search for security and reach out to the risk of living with both arms. One has to embrace the world like a lover. One has to accept pain as a condition of existence. One has to court doubt and darkness as the cost of knowing. One needs a will stubborn in conflict, but apt always to total acceptance of every consequence of living and dying.

Harvest Summary for Chapter 4: Live and Let Live

Chapter 5
Bear Sweet Fruit

Introduction

Likable people are positive thinkers who tend to be helpful and have a good sense of humor. They have a way of making everyone feel comfortable, relaxed, no matter what the activity. These caring people show enthusiastic interest in all others, family, friends, acquaintances, and strangers. In their presence, no one remains a stranger for long. They generously listen and help whomever they can. Those who love them understand it is best not to get in the way of their giving. They seem to get great joy in giving little, unexpected presents. They bear sweet fruit.

My godmother Mary Ann is one of the likable people in my life. When I was making my first trip to Europe, she not only sent me spending money, but also scoured the stores until she found the perfect card depicting my nine-year-old dog's sentiments about being without me for twenty-one days, our longest separation. When I returned I found on my machine her message telling me she was

The Likable Qualities Exercise 1

For this exercise, take a sheet of paper and draw a line vertically down the middle. Now write at the top of the left side: The things I do so that people will like me. Then, write at the top of the right side: The things other people do that makes me like them.

Save your paper. You can compare the traits you wrote down with the traits in the next exercise.

The Likable Qualities Exercise 2

Part of every relationship-building class I teach takes participants through creating a list of the qualities they like about others. While each new class duplicates many of the traits, every once in a while, I get to add a new one or two. Currently I have a list of 30 characteristics that make people likable:

thinking of me and saying she was anxious to hear all about my trip.

I've also noticed, and you probably have, too, that most likable people are the least demanding and the most accepting. That doesn't mean they aren't assertive and able to ask for what they want. They just seem to need their way less often than offensive people.

Likeable people, I find share these three global characteristics. They tend to be more simple than complex which makes them easy to understand, consistent, and comfortable to be around. In addition, you'll find them almost infinitely patient with you, themselves, and life in general. Their patience helps you feel relaxed when you are with them, unhurried, unpressured, less tense, and accepted. Finally, likable people are broadly compassionate. Their gentle forgiving nature allows them to be understanding when people act out of character. Indeed, they have the grace to generally believe that people are acting out of character whenever they behave badly.

Likable people also manage a challenging balance between humility and high self-esteem. When I saw this win-win combination time and again in likable people, it helped me redefine humility in my own mind.

If you want to be generally liked by most people, learn to understand humility from this connecting definition: *To be humble is not to think little of myself, on the contrary, it is to think much of myself AND others as well.*

In my definition, self-esteem is a close cousin of humility. Because self-esteem has become so popular a subject over the last several years, I share this basic definition: *People with high self-esteem continually develop and maintain a strong sense of personal worth as they relate to themselves and others.*

When you have genuine self-esteem and authentic humility, you are then, and only then, a truly powerful person. Likable people attain tremendous power and as wide an influence as they seek. Will Rogers, a popular pop philosopher, said, "I never met a . . . [person] I didn't like."

In this chapter you'll learn how to develop your positive attitude, serve others without wearing yourself out, and sharpen your sense of humor, gaining the three character traits universally shared by happy, likable people.

Positive Attitude, Bloom Where Planted

Wherever you are, whomever you meet, whatever situation you find

Committed
Compassionate
Confident
Courageous
Decisive—Clear about Likes and Dislikes
Dedicated
Determined
Express Thoughts Clearly
Fun
Generous
Goal-Oriented
Honest
Intelligent
Non-Judgmental
Nurturing
Patient
Positive Attitude
Reliable
Respectful of All People
Responsible
See Bigger Picture
Similar Interests
Think Things Through and Plan Things Out
Trustworthy
Sense of Humor
Sensitive to Others
Smile a Lot
Spiritually Connected
Straight Forward
Willing to Do Whatever it Takes

Did you find a number of these traits on the lists

you prepared in the first exercise?

For this exercise, check off on the left the traits you believe you already have or that others have said you have. If you checked all of them, you no doubt are a wonderfully popular human being with your family, friends, and most people you meet. If you didn't check all of them, go back and look at those qualities you didn't check. Carefully choose no more than three you wish you possessed, and check them off on the right. Commit to achieving them over the next year. Go back again and again each year until you master them all.

Please honor yourself and make realistic goals. If you choose more than three new traits, you are less likely to succeed in creating these new behaviors. Failing a goal doesn't feel good, and prevents you from acquiring traits that make you more likable.

yourself in, you have freedom of choice to choose your attitude and choose your action. Bloom where planted speaks to making the best choices among the options available to you each time, every time.

Positive attitude speaks to looking for the good in everything. Some call it *optimism.* For some, positive attitude is a natural gift, along with a sunny disposition. If a positive attitude does not come naturally to you, take heart. You can improve your outlook and even small improvements can have a big impact. Think about this possibility—What if nothing good happened naturally and you had to make all good things happen for yourself? I believe this is essentially true. People create their own realities, tend to get what they expect.

The way you are, mostly positive or mostly negative, affects others, everyone you interact with. You may never have thought about how much power your attitude has on others. You know what you feel like after an encounter with a negative person. Without a powerful inner core of joy and peace, a negative person can pluck the bloom off your happiness and leave you feeling spent.

When you meet people with a positive attitude, you feel good about your interaction. They have a positive presence and sprinkle their conversations with laughter, love, and joy. There is really no reason why you can't acquire such a positive attitude, once you make up your mind to have one.

Joy does not come from things, but rather lies within where people and things may increase the joy already there. David Steindl-Rast said, "Joy is the happiness that does not depend on what happens." I believe, comparatively, Positive attitude is the state of mind that doesn't depend on what happens.

Positive self-esteem, a pleasant image of yourself, seems an essential trait if you are to maintain a positive attitude no matter what bad news befalls you. When you think about it, what sense does a negative stance make? Look at your pessimistic beliefs as bad habits and examine them like a detective. Look for evidence to support them. When you find support lacking, resolve to replace them with positive beliefs.

Healthy self-esteem is a good habit that enables you and tells you that you can do what you set out to do. Self-esteem bundled with a positive attitude, maintains your mental stamina to ride out setbacks and direct hits. Poor self-esteem, conversely, is a bad habit that works to self-sabotage, preventing you from believing in your ability to achieve your goals. Your self image is

Offensive Traits That Make People Unpopular Exercise 3

Whenever I take my class through this exercise, I always find that participants come up with far fewer things they don't like about others than what they do like. The energy in the room gets very different as well. With the likable qualities, the energy is up, good, and people smile. With this exercise, it seems harder for each person to think of more than one or two things that really bother them about others. When I took myself through this exercise with a class, I found I had the same experience as they had. I, like my class participants, don't spend nearly as much time with people I don't like. That's probably why the offensive qualities don't come as easily. Here are the nine offensive behaviors that come up most often in my classes:

–Tell Only Half the Story
–Usually Arrive Late
–Chameleons Who Change depending on Whom They are With
–People Who are Inflexible once They Make a Decision
–Know-It-Alls
–People Who are Part of the Problem And Won't Own It
–Anal Retentives
–People Who are Poor Priority Setters
–People Who Don't or Won't Talk

On the left side check off the offensive behaviors you don't believe are a problem for you. On the right side check off the one offensive behavior you want to change now. Please choose only one offensive behavior to change at a time. Changing a bad habit is harder than acquiring a new behavior. Changing a bad habit requires new seeding. First, you have to dig out the roots of the bad behavior and remove them. Next, you have to

the photograph of yourself you carry in your heart and mind.

Think about the person you wrote about in the exercise as if that person were a character in a novel. How would you rate their attitude on a scale of 1-10, 1 meaning a negative attitude and 10 meaning a positive attitude?

You may be feeling uncomfortable with this probing exercise. Some of you may even have a negative attitude about having too positive an attitude. I've heard positive people called Pollyanna's, and Dummies in Denial. This Optimist Creed, whose authorship I do not know, may help you see positive attitude in a different light—

Optimists maintain a healthy attitude about themselves, others, and life. Optimists believe they deserve happiness. Their positive attitude pushes them to seek the good kernels from everything that happens to them.

Make no mistake: maintaining a positive attitude can challenge. Yet the alternative, negative attitude, is ever horrible, like an open invitation for trouble to infest your every waking hour.

I ask you this question about positive attitude: if not now, when? At first it will feel strange looking for those kernels of good, the experiences, the lessons. Yet, with each reinforcement of your commitment to developing a positive attitude habit, you build your mental toughness. Remember the *fake it until you make it* philosophy. Those of you who think faking it is a philosophy for phonies, remember how you learned to talk, walk, and use the toilet in a civilized manner. You began from a point of not knowing how, to a point of knowing how. Rather than phony, *fake it until you make it* is actually the way we learn everything new.

You work at your positive attitude mechanically, awkwardly at first, like walking. With each new step you do a bit better, feel a bit more stable. Then, like a beginning shoot with its two tiny leaves, you grow. You build and build until your positive attitude gets downright bushy in its growth.

prepare yourself to accept and act on the new behavior. Only then can change really happen. Unless you dig out the roots of the bad behavior, the established behavior will choke off the fragile new behavior.

My Photograph of Myself Exercise

Think about what you look like to you on the inside. Write down how you feel about your abilities?
Then, answer these questions:
How happy are you with your life today?
If you were successful in your own eyes, what would that look like to you?

Promise Yourself

To be so strong that nothing can disturb your peace of mind.

To talk health, happiness, and prosperity to every person you meet.

To make all your friends feel that there is something in them.

To look at the sunny side of everything and make your optimism come true.

To think only of the best, to work only for the best, and expect only the best.

To be just as enthusiastic about the success of others as you are about your own.

Here's a prayer for strength from Dr. Norman Vincent Peale: *Our heavenly Father, we ask You to bless us and give us that insight and that greatness of spirit by which we can stand up to life's problems. We give You thanks through Jesus Christ our Lord. Amen.*

Did you catch the positive attitude statement at the end? Dr. Peale's prayer thanks God for answered prayer in the same breath as the prayer itself.

This year, I decided to catch up with technology in a big way with two concurrent projects. The first project replaced my entertainment system that included an 8-track tape player, 45 and 33-1/3 record player, 15-year-old television, and 11-year-old VCR. The second replaced my 386 computer and 15-year old printer.

When the entertainment group came in, the CD player refused to function in continuous play. The AM/FM radio would only play FM audibly. The television needed a $100 booster to bring in the stations. The radio needed a booster to bring in AM reception. The day after installation, a windstorm blew away reception to six of the seven stations I receive. Just when I thought everything was resolved, my television screen developed a huge, black square in the center of the picture on all channels.

While I dealt with this nonworking technology, I discovered an insurance company had cut off benefits without notice, had investigators following me around, videotaping me. One investigator infiltrated my class using fake credentials and made most of my students uneasy.

In addition, the Dow Jones industrial average dropped a whopping 500 points during the same month and I lost 25 percent of my nest egg built from years of growth.

Then my computer equipment came in. The docking station buzzed and had to be replaced. The fax program would neither send nor receive. The keyboard stopped working when the manufacturer's technician took me through diagnostics. The scanner would not install. One software installation caused malfunctions in my mouse, modem, fax program, and operating system. The laptop and docking station needed to be reordered and replaced.

A few days later, I fell while walking the dog and hurt my ankle, knees, hip, hand, ribs, cut open my mouth, and bruised my cheek.

Finally, a power surge sent my gas range into a series of blips, beeps, and failure code.

Haven't you had periods like this? What do you do when your life goes through a hurricane of chaos? Are you wondering how anyone can maintain a positive attitude when their world is a chaotic disaster? Here is my Mix And Match Nine-Point Formula For Maintaining A Positive Attitude:

Hold a Global Prospective—How bad off am I compared to those who are the worst off in the world? People in Third World countries would likely consider my problems relatively minor compared to their struggles. The children who eat, receive medical care, clothing, and education on $24 a month have no electricity. Remember also to keep track of the good things that happen during chaotic times. For me, I lost my wallet and found it in a fifteen-minute time frame. I got the call that Thomas More wanted to publish this book. Keeping a positive prospective is a bit like this story:

Tessa had a new baby brother. Every day
Tessa would ask her parents if she could talk
with her baby brother all by herself. Her parents
were hesitant. Tessa persisted and they finally gave in.
They had a monitor and they listened.
Tessa asked her baby brother, "Sean,
tell me about God. I'm starting to forget."

Hold a Personal Prospective—How Important is this problem within the overall context of my life? Of all the components within the entertainment system, the CD player rose to top priority because I listen to music when I write. At minimum, an AM/FM radio ought to be able to play both frequencies at least decently. Comparatively, most of the television channels should come in reasonably well. The store worked with me to do the best it could do and we both moved on. The computer is necessary for my work. Objective reality says new technology is complicated, has bugs, can be slow. I need to increase my knowledge so I can intelligently and aggressively problem-solve and feel less scared and helpless. Protecting financial stability is important. Cooking equipment is important. Minor injuries are less important.

Follow the Wisdom in St. Francis' *Serenity Prayer*: *God grant me the Serenity to accept the things I cannot change . . . courage to change the things I can . . . and the Wisdom to know the difference. Amen.* The issues St. Francis addressed are two and I phrase them into questions I ask myself. *Who owns the problem? Do I have the power to change the situation?* My mother taught me this St. Francis wisdom which she lived every day of her life.

In each of the six situations, I owned the problem and had total control of my attitude that I was determined to keep positive. However, my control was limited in most other aspects of each of the situations. The technology in the entertainment and computer systems as well as the stove were outside of my control. I had little control over the fall of the stock market or my fall. Insurance and private investigators I discovered can broadly invade your privacy using creative lies and false identities to gather information from you, your family, friends, neighbors, and coworkers, including following and videotaping you without your permission. Investigators take advantage of people's natural desire to help. Think about it. If someone came to you and said a family member or friend gave you their name as a reference, would you speak with them before you called and verified that what the stranger said was true? Most people wouldn't. The police can't protect you because there is no suspicion of criminal activity. No one is forced to give private investigators information, but whatever information they gather is usable. If they could not freely invade people's privacy, they would have no information to sell.

Keep Your Focus on What You Can Do, Not What You Can't Do—In any situation, lay out your options as you would a harvest display. In seeking all options ask yourself two questions: *What can I do? Who or what could help me?* Multiply yourself whenever possible. In every one of the situations, I actively helped myself and enlisted others' help. First I called every prayer line. Help came from three large corporations, two state regulatory agencies, one consultant, and three lawyers.

Follow the Wisdom of Joshua When Taking Action: Be strong and courageous. *Do not be terrified; do not be discouraged, for the Lord your God will be with you wherever you go.* (1:9 NIV)

The power of a positive attitude manifests in greater objectivity and the ability to see the bigger picture and ask, *What is the highest and best use of my time?* For the entertainment center, accepting that some channels would not come in perfectly made sense. I accepted that I needed to be gentle with myself during the healing process after the fall. After doing some historical research, I decided to trust my portfolio managers and ride out the storm. With the computer system, since I could still write, I decided to trust the professional technicians to get all the components of the system running as quickly as they could. I negotiated with the stove manufacturer and got a 25 percent reduction in the cost of a new stove, along with a 10 percent store discount. Because my privacy is a sensitive issue with me, I requested the regulatory authorities to mediate on my behalf with the insurance company.

Keep Soldiering On With a Positive Attitude—This is my Global Prospective Mantra: *I am a happy person with a good life who creatively solves my problems.* My mother had sayings that help me when I'm in the thick of things, *Keep putting one foot in front of the other and you'll get where you're going* and *Take one day at a time.*

Seek Out the Gift within the Trouble—I have many more options with my new computer system and my state of the art entertainment system with gloriously improved sound. When my portfolio dropped, I held tight instead of selling off everything like I did in October 1987, much to my financial benefit. With the insurance company, I was able to fight the good fight with help, but let go of the outcome. My fall made me grateful nothing had broken. The stove breakdown made me proud of my negotiating skills and thankful that the breakdown did not occur on Thanksgiving when I was cooking my first turkey dinner in years.

Fight Off Negative Dialogue, both Internally and Externally—Replace the negative, gloom and doom dialog that comes into your head with repetitive positive contradictions. I react when people say things like: *You're really having a bad day. You must be getting a cold. You have the worst luck. You're always falling. Nothing ever works right for you.* I refuse to accept their negative prognoses. Instead, I tell them, *What an awful thing to say to me. I don't believe it for a minute.* Yes, I get some strange reactions, and they rarely say them to me again.

Maintain Your Focus—Nothing can remain stagnant against the onslaught of the strength of focused concentration and action.

There is a Hasidic saying, *When you walk across the fields with your mind pure and holy, then from all the stones and all growing things and all animals, the spoils of their souls come out and cling to you, and then they are purified and become a holy fire in you.*

You may be wondering how to keep a positive attitude when troubles keep coming at you one right after the other. One thing to remember is, *If you look for imperfections, you're likely to find them.*

Here's a story whose author is unknown—

An avid duck hunter was in the market for a new dog. His search ended when he found a dog that could actually walk on water to retrieve a duck. Shocked by his find, he was sure none of his friends would ever believe him. He decided to try to break the news to a friend of his, a pessimist by nature, and invited him to hunt with him and his new dog.

As they waited by the shore, a flock of ducks flew by. They fired and a duck fell. The dog responded and jumped into the water. The dog, however, did not sink but instead walked across the water to retrieve the bird, never getting more than his four paws wet.

The friend saw everything but did not say a single word. On the drive home the hunter asked his friend, "Did you notice anything unusual about my dog?"

"I sure did," responded his friend. "He can't swim."

Recognize that moving from poor me negativity to good life positivity begins in an extremely mechanical way. When troubles besiege you, it's natural to feel down. Your energy gets low, and all you seem to want to think about are your troubles. When you want to move yourself out of the doldrums, plan on working at it for 15-20 minutes in the beginning. When you get stuck in problem mode, getting out is hard work, especially when the problem is still blooming. You may feel like I am telling you, *Don't think about a pink elephant.*

Think of your mind like a silo. If you have it full of problems, you have no room for solutions. Begin by replacing problem thoughts with solution thoughts. Make your mind a problem solver instead of a problem holder. This is mechanical. Every time the problem buzzes back into your mind, swat it out with thoughts of the outcome you want. You may truly feel ridiculous at first. And you need to do it anyway. Act as if you can swat your problems out of your mind with solution visualizations. Remember the retired couple needing to gain a farmers' mindset to succeed as farmers. You need a solution mindset to succeed in solving your problems. Remember walking away may be your best solution in some instances. Always ask, *is this a good use of my time and/or money.*

The Hurricane of Chaos Exercise

My hurricane of challenges is hardly unique. You probably can tell your own story of more sour apples than sweet falling before you. Like me, you've developed ways to survive strings of challenges, some better than others.

Think of the most recent string of challenging situations that gave you a run for your money. Put them in chronological order as I did above. Then answer these questions:

How did you cope with all the stress?

How did you deal with each challenge?

How much help did you seek or get offered to you?

What happened to let you know you were ready to move on from the problem or situation?

Right now you are coming to an exciting moment. You have been preparing for this moment throughout the book, giving yourself the gift of imperturbability. You now have the knowledge you need to become an unflappable human being. You've learned you can only control your own behavior. You have learned that expression does and suppression hides. This is where you put it all together and find your freedom-giving mental center of gravity. Viktor Frankl exemplified this freedom in his book *Man's Search for Meaning*. Frankl taught me how to choose my attitude and response in any given situation. Here's my adaptation of one of Frankl's stories:

> *The German officers came to Frankl's cell in the concentration camp and took him into an interrogation room. They told him he had some information they would be willing to exchange for his freedom. Frankl told them, "What you offer me is my liberty. I have my freedom. I will always have my freedom. No one could ever take my freedom away from me."*

Up until now you have concentrated on gaining a dependable and consistent positive attitude. Once you have a positive attitude, you need to actively do some positive programming every day to keep it. Each morning, for example, I proclaim out loud, "Today is going to be a great day!" Then I use motivational speaker, Dave Yoho's morning programming, *I am a unique and precious being created by God for very special purposes. This day belongs to me and no one can take it away. God has placed me on this journey and He will care for me until its end.*

In addition, I created an attitude acronym I named The Winning Attitude:

A is for Action-Oriented

T is for Teach What You Know

T is for Think Positively

I is for I Like Me

T is for Take Time to Love Yourself, Others, and Life

U is for Understand Yourself, Others, and Life

D is for Deal Directly with Yourself, Others, and Life

E is for Educate Yourself, Learning Something New Every Day

These positive steps help you stay unflappable, resistant, and imperturbable to the point where no one and no thing can disturb your inner core of joy and peace. Along the way to building a core of joy and peace, positive thinkers build tolerances for the pesky disturbances of life. Out of a coaching introduction on the subject of tolerance, my curiosity caused me to list things, 28 things, I choose to tolerate without making a fuss:

- ❖ Views different from mine without need for debate
- ❖ The way things are instead of the way I want them to be
- ❖ First-time mistakes
- ❖ Accidents as a part of life, my own and others
- ❖ All levels of maturity, regardless of age
- ❖ My own imperfections
- ❖ Dog washing after wet walks

- Medicine when absolutely necessary
- Unexpected wet dog in my lap
- Getting needles for medication and testing
- Middle of the night doggy nature calls
- Dog barking
- Dog hair
- Unavoidable episodes of waiting in lines
- Rejection
- Dog's agenda vs. my agenda
- Dirt on the porch
- Winter
- Stupid things I do without thinking
- Seeds in black grapes and pomegranates
- Oil separation in nut butters
- Laws I must obey
- People who don't say *Thank you*
- Water as healthy beverage of choice
- Calorie management
- Optimists can segregate a problem from other areas of their lives while pessimists let a problem spill into and spoil every other area of their lives.
- Optimists see good fortune as a reward while pessimists see good fortune as an accident.
- Optimists are able to put their burdens down while pessimists carry their burdens wherever they go.

How harmful is negative thinking? On average, 77 percent of everything people think is negative and 75 percent of all illnesses are self-induced. Motivational speaker, Brian Tracy said, "You need to talk

to yourself all the time." Ninety percent of your emotion comes from inner dialogue, and the key is to explain things to yourself in a positive way.

It is cold, dark, and cluttered inside negative thinking minds. Negative thinkers try to hide their fears with addictions, depression, guilt, procrastination, and shyness. Picture these mind monsters and emotional traps lurking in your mental landscape:

Wicked Witch/Warlock—Your critical/judgmental voice inside that keeps telling you what a rotter you are, over and over making fun of who you are and what you do

Cold Dark Moor—Emotional confusion that causes bad decisions or paralyzes you

Rushing White Water—overflowing emotions like fear, sadness, and anxiety

Quicksand—Depression

Alligator-Infested Swamp—Addiction/substance abuse

Oz Yellow Brick Road—Unfulfilled desires

Desert—Scarcity thinking

Positive thinkers know that they can stop their pain, that life doesn't have to hurt. James M. Barrie said, "The secret of happiness is not in doing what one likes, but in liking what one has to do." The positive thinker lives Ken Blanchard's one minute attitude adjuster, *In one minute I can change my attitude and in that minute I can change my entire day.*

Once you feel comfortably positive in your attitudes and thinking, you may forget to pay attention to your negative mental static. When negative thoughts buzz around in your head, you can forget to swat them and replace them with repetitive positive thoughts. Some negative thought processes come cleverly disguised. You want your loved ones to mark your birthday as a special occasion, an exciting event. Yet, your mind plays a movie over and over that they forget your birthday. You berate yourself for making such a big thing out of

The Things I Tolerate Exercise

Set a timer for 15 minutes. The number of things you write down for this exercise is less important than consciously looking at the things you choose to tolerate.

your birthday. What you want and what you imagine are opposites.

Lester Levensen said that desire is an admission of lack. The premise states what you want you obviously don't have. In the birthday example, if a celebration is important to you, make sure you create one that suits you. If other fun things come your way, that's a bonus. If you place the success or failure of your birthday in the hands of others, you turn a day that is important to you into an unharvested crop.

What saves the positive person's day and what destroys the negative person's day are often opposites:

> Optimists' problems are temporary, while pessimists' problems are permanent.

Positive thinkers are like fresh green shoots that bounce back when bent by the wind and careless feet. Negative thinkers are like brittle, old twigs that lack the resilience to snap back when bent. *Blessed are the flexible for they will not be bent out of shape.* Positive thinkers flex and bend, try new things, persist until they succeed, take risks, and focus on the positive outcomes they want. This functions in their lives like positive programming. Positive thinkers live in a positive world. Negative thinkers are rigid, give up more easily, and focus on what they don't want to happen. This functions in their lives like negative programming. Negative thinkers live in a negative world.

Positive thinkers also have an attitude of gratitude and feel thankful for the things that do go their way and give them pleasure. Remember my hurricane of chaos. I felt grateful for my miracle of getting my wallet back in tact so fast I could pay the postage on my packages. I loved meeting a teenager with such a beautiful character that his joy came from finding the owner. He absolutely refused to take any reward. How kind it was for the manufacturer who bought out the manufacturer of my range to offer to reimburse me 25 percent of the price of a new stove and advise me that it would be foolish to put more money in my existing stove. Then, there were the three lawyers in three states who advised me freely about my insurance company problems without charge. My computer consultant feels like my own personal Steadfast Tin Soldier. Each one of my holistic practitioners worked hard to get my bruised body back into shape. Finally, I felt grateful that I had the ability to walk away from some of the problems and get on with my life. Some problems aren't worth the time and money it takes to solve them.

Blooming where you are planted is all about having the determination to grow and blossom no matter what tries to stop you. The wind beneath the wings of your determination is a positive attitude. Positive thinking people are consistently reasonable, see the big picture, and avoid the negative traps that spoil days and sometimes lives. Maintaining a positive attitude is like choosing to walk in the sunshine instead of moping around in a fog.

Be a Good Neighbor

Mother Teresa captured the essence of volunteering when she said, "Let us not be satisfied with just giving money; money can be got; but they need your hearts to love them."

I like The National Volunteer Center's logo, a triangle with a heart at the top and reads, *Volunteers—Hearts at Work!*

What calls people to volunteer? Most people lead busy lives, have any number of people and things vying for their time. How do they fit in volunteer activities? Some do it for the joy it brings them. Mihaly Csikszenthmilaly said, "Strange as it may seem, life becomes serene and enjoyable precisely when selfish pleasure and personal success are no longer the guiding goals."

Here are some of the benefits you receive when you volunteer from your heart in the spirit of goodness:

- You feel useful, needed.
- You know that you are giving back something to the world in gratitude for what has been given to you.
- You can put your own struggles and challenges in perspective when you see how challenged some others are.
- You find good homes for all the things you don't need, including extra money.
- Sharing your love brings you a beautiful joy.
- You gain a positive citizen image.
- You grow personally from selfless service and sacrifice.
- Volunteering builds self-worth and self-esteem.
- The spiritual rewards are endless.

Adults, I find, tend to volunteer for four reasons:

- Fill Up Their Time.
- Social Reasons—Seek visibility to gain recognition for their efforts, meet people, learn people and organization skills, and further their careers through their volunteer activity network.
- Feel Useful—Have a need to do worthwhile work in the world, to make efforts that count for something.
- Genuine Caring For The Needs Of Others.

Three of the reasons are self-centered and one is other-centered. Certainly, many people will choose to pursue volunteer activites for a combination of these reasons. For those whose volunteer activities call them from their hearts, their world is one they make a better place with their efforts. When you consider 49 percent of adults and 59 percent of teenagers volunteer an average of 218 hours annually, you begin to understand how much helping gets done in America. America's 106 million volunteers work 22.7 billion hours for others and their labor is estimated at a value of $209.2 billion.

The happiest people I know serve others in a myriad of ways. Their loving empathy spreads beyond their family and friends to wherever they find a need they can address.

I relocated to upstate New York while my family and friends remained scattered in every state but New York. The second Thanksgiving here an unexpected overnight snow storm prevented me from traveling to see my family in Pennsylvania. The dog and I ate ham sandwiches and walked along deserted streets. It was the only Thanksgiving when I didn't get my favorite pumpkin pie. I felt unfamilied that morning of my first non-family Thanksgiving holiday. Then I took hold of myself and, some of you may have guessed, I used Third World perspective to re-center myself in joy and peace. Merlin and I went to Stewart's and enjoyed a cone of pumpkin ice cream. After I told that story, every year early in November two friends, Pat and Charlotte, make it a point to invite me to their family's Thanksgiving gatherings. Their commitment to me is so strong I am invited even when their families are invited out. I spent one Thanksgiving with Pat and her wonderful family the year a snow storm prevented me from traveling to see my family.

Another time, four feet of fresh snow fell in March over three feet of old snow. I heard noise coming from the closed-off guest room just before leaving for church. To my horror I found a half-inch of ice frozen over my hardwood floors. The mattresses below the skylight were soaked from the steady stream of water dripping from the corners of my flat roof's skylight. I put a bucket and pot under the dripping and went to church. I told my elderly neighbors, Bob and Mary, what was happening at my house. Bob said: "Don't worry about it. I'll come over in the truck with a ladder and go up on the roof and see what I can do."

Within an hour after climbing onto my roof, my skinny 80-year old knight had chipped away drains through the ice. Water was pouring off the roof. Then he started throwing huge blocks of ice off the roof. These blocks of ice were so huge they cracked the sidewalk below. *Where did he get the strength?* I asked him while writing this book. He said, *we can do a lot of things when we have to. Besides, I didn't really pick them up, I just pushed them off with the ice pick.*

I thought about what he said and I went outside and measured. The distance between my house wall and the cracked sidewalk spans 11 feet. I believe I had two miracles that scary Sunday morning, the miracle of a caring volunteer and whatever force lifted those ice boulders 11 feet from the house. Those two miracles saved my roof that day.

Volunteers nourish and heal people with their compassion.

Do you feel you would like to do more volunteering but hesitate to make even short term commitments? Fear of overextending yourself may stop you from jumping onto the volunteer band wagon. Here are some of the reasons people don't volunteer more:

- ❖ Don't have the free time or money
- ❖ Feel busy helping the needy within their own families
- ❖ Don't know who to contact
- ❖ Want to avoid getting on lists and receiving endless telephone and written pleas
- ❖ Worry that groups will pressure them to do more than they really want to
- ❖ Feel skittish because of scams
- ❖ Want to remain anonymous because they can't say *no*

A volunteer activity is an unpaid job. Accept it responsibly. Ask questions. Set parameters. Let the organization or the individual know how much time you can commit to contribute. Find out if the organization provides third-party liability insurance for its volunteers. If you use your automobile or your home for volunteer activities, ask your insurance agent if your automobile, homeowners, or umbrella/excess insurance policies provide coverage for your volunteer activities.

The happiest, most fulfilled volunteers look for groups or situations that tug at their hearts: children, animals, the elderly, the sick, the dying, or are drawn to cultural or political volunteer activities. These proactive volunteers control their activities and help in ways that appeal to them.

Martin Luther King, Jr. said that *every man must decide whether . . . [to] walk in the light of creative altruism or in the darkness of destructive selfishness*. This is the judgment. Life's most urgent question is what are you doing for others?

When you want to match yourself with a volunteer activity, consider your skills. Can you sit quietly and listen? Then perhaps Hospice, which helps the dying leave this world with dignity, could be your volunteer home. Do you like a one-on-one helping relationship? Then, Big Brothers, Big Sisters, foster grandparents, or sports coaching may be for you. Are you more comfortable joining a volunteer organization? Then, you may consider Soroptimists, The Lions Club, Points of Light Foundation, or religious houses of worship as good matches for you. You may be someone who likes to go it alone and help and volunteer as you see need. Perhaps you would rather contribute than volunteer.

Here are some ways you can make sure you enjoy your volunteer activities:

- Decide whether you prefer a leadership or support role.
- Choose only organizations or activities you believe in.
- Consider making volunteering a family activity.
- Make volunteering a learning experience by taking Hospice, ski patrol, Neighborhood Watch, firefighter or Emergency Medical Technician training.
- Make supporting charities an entertainment activity by attending dinners, dances, auctions, or other events.

I have never met a happy person who did not serve others freely, lovingly, and frequently. Volunteers get a helper's high that makes them feel good physically, emotionally, and spiritually. They often

Good Works Exercise

Question 1: In what capacities do you volunteer your time?

What can you think of that you did during the last year as a volunteer, a good neighbor, to help a friend, family member, your house of worship, schools, or in service to the poor. You may be surprised at how much you do when you take time to write it out.

Question 2: To what charities do you contribute? Remember to include all the times you reach into your pocket or purse for spontaneous giving.

connect with people they help in a special way. They volunteer for the love of humankind, to lend muscle and mind to the needy. They tithe themselves.

I had a neighbor who was born on the Fourth of July in 1899. A few years after I arrived, she moved into a nursing home against her will. I would visit her with my dog, Merlin the Magician. As I entered her room, I'd see her roommate in her wheel chair motionless with her chin in her chest. As soon as she saw Merlin, she would pick her head right up and tell me, *I used to have a little dog,* all the while smiling at Merlin. I'd ask her if she would like to pet him. Sometimes she would take him into her lap. Mabel enjoyed him, too. The last day I saw Mabel, I took her out of her room into the sunny courtyard in a lounge chair on wheels. She enjoyed seeing the family of newborn ducks that had nested in the corner of the building. Then she laughed out loud as she watched Merlin and me playing with a huge beach ball. When I saw her son in church, he told me Mabel had died. I told him the story of our last day together and he was stunned. *My mother hadn't recognized any of us for a month before she died.* Merlin's magic or lucid miracle, who can say? I was sure glad Merlin and I could make Mabel laugh and bring her some joy my last day with her.

HONE YOUR FUNNY BONE

Humor is an incredibly important social skill. If you want to get along, get laughs. Funny takes are like soft, rubber bumpers around the sharp edges of life. Robert Weider said that once you have them by the funny bone, their hearts and minds will follow.

A sense of humor is a terrific personality trait to have. Every popular person I know laughs a lot, teases, and makes fun. When you choose to look for the laughs, you affirm life.

Bishop Fulton J. Sheen said that laughter is the juxtaposition of two ideas. He told a story on his popular television show about a little girl and her family having dinner with the local priest. The priest asked the child, "What are you going to do when you get big like your mommy?" *Diet,* she responded.

Marriage is two funny things staying together for the laughs trying to remember whatever made them decide it would be a good idea for them to live together. A family is a group of funny things vying for dibs on the smallest room in the house. Work is a group of funny characters functioning without a plot who tend to thicken in the middle. Church is a funny mix of the strange, the straight, and the spiritual all trying to figure out why some ancient homeless guy loved them enough to leave them a legacy.

I belong to The Society for the Ladies Who Laugh Out Loud and founder, Katherine Lyons Bridge, gave me a message bookmark that said, *it takes 13 muscles to smile and 50 muscles to frown. Stay young. Practice turning the corners up.* The Society's number is 207-967-4676 and there are chapters is many states. Start your own and invite people to Laugh Lunches. I have also graduated from the University of Light Hearts in 1994 with my degree in Laughing. On the Official U.L.H. Alumni Association membership card, university president, Daphne G. Triphon, put the following Three Star Daily Pledge:

I pledge to pursue laughter in my daily life.

I pledge to have a light heart daily just for the health of it.

I pledge to be grateful for one new thing daily.

The average six-year-old laughs 300 times a day and the average adult laughs 7-8 times. Do you laugh 7-8 times each day? Do you ever have days when you laugh 300 times? For optimum health an adult should laugh 40-60 times a day. I believe the more you laugh the happier you feel. E-mail is quickly catching on as an easy way to send funny stories to groups of people you think would enjoy them. I get them from my youngest daughter, my cousin in Pennsylvania, my friend in Canada. I send and get cartoons and funny stories by regular mail.

My Aunt Peggy is a good example of someone who has laughed her way through life. Whenever I think of her I can hear her laughter. When people are with her, pretty soon everyone is laughing. At seventy-five she still works. Her boss says, *She is always pleasant, congenial, never complains about anything. You'd never know she ever had a trouble in her world. And her laugh rings through this office and just brightens your day.*

All people have pain in their lives, but whether they choose to suffer through it or smile through it is an option. Leo Buscaglia said that when you're at the end of your rope, tie a knot at the end of it and swing.

When I had the accident in my forties that ended my career, life became really hard for me. My body didn't even have enough energy to digest food. I needed something to turn the tide quickly and I watched or listened to every funny tape I could get my hands on, read every funny book I could find, even children's joke books. Every once in a while something would hit me just right, and I would get a good belly laugh. Throughout the day I would think of it and laugh all over again.

I also have a mental file of pictures of funny things. The classic is the Tidy Bowl Man. Years ago, there was a commercial with this Tidy Bowl Man rowing a boat around the toilet tank. I literally fell on the floor laughing the first time I saw it. Another is of my Victorian-mannered mother with chocolate and marshmallow candy on all her fingers and all over her face walking in the mall desperately trying to clean herself with tissues. Of course the more she tried to clean off the worse the mess became. She had white tissue paper stuck to every one of her fingers, parts of her face, and her handbag. The Stan Laurel look she gave my hysterical daughters and me before she disappeared into the Ladies Room became the photo for my mental funny file.

I literally grew up laughing. Each of my parents came from large families who visited often. Squeezed around the dinette table, they told funny stories. One birthday dinner, my Uncle Pete laughed so hard a big, fat noodle came out of his nose. Lots of people have said that was anatomically impossible. I saw it. I can still see it and it still makes me laugh. It's another one of my mental funny photos.

Proverbs 17:22 states, *A merry heart doeth good like medicine...*" Both of my parents had the gift of seeing and laughing at life's absurdities and people's quirks, including their own. My father was a kidder who also told jokes, coined funny sayings, and kept everyone around him in stitches. (In case you haven't been laughing much lately, stitches are those pains you get in your sides when you laugh too hard for too long.) He called little children *Banana Noses*. One three-year-old noticed my father's huge Italian nose and retorted, "Have you ever looked at your nose?" We all broke out into such loud, spontaneous laughter it scared him and he cried as hard as we were laughing.

My mother had a drier sense of humor. When I was a young teenager, the neighborhood kids started sneaking out their windows on summer nights to play midnight hide and seek. It was great fun. On the third night, as I climbed out my window, I saw my mother's face. *Going some place?*

I'm chasing a mosquito.

I already killed it. Go back to bed.

The humorous household tradition continues in both my home and my brother's. Once when my youngest daughter and I couldn't see eye to eye, I began my usual—taking on the lighter side of the situation. She started to laugh. Desperately trying to stop herself from

The What Makes You Laugh? Exercise

Have you ever thought about what kind of a sense of humor you have? I invite you to poke around and check out the part humor plays in your life.

Write down your funniest personal story.

Write down what happened the last time you laughed at yourself.

When was the last time you had a full belly laugh? Why did what happened strike you so funny?

Who are you with when you laugh the most? What is it about the two of you together that makes for so much fun?

What is your preferred humor: short, one-liners, slap stick, visual, funny stories, satire, situation comedy?

Who thinks you're funny? Why? (If you don't know, ask them.)

What is your funniest family story?

laughing, she yelled, "Stop making me laugh when I'm mad." Of course, that made us all laugh. Ralph Waldo Emerson said, "If you want to rule the world you must keep it amused."

The best humor is situational, creative, clean humor that creates fun without putting anyone down, humor that heals instead of hurts.

In Buffalo, New York, at a business meeting in a large restaurant, about fifteen of us found ourselves waiting and waiting for our order to come. By the time our wait approached an hour, one of the women showed us how she could balance a spoon on her nose. Before long most of us had learned and someone got the idea to march around the restaurant with spoons and forks hanging from our noses, cheeks and chins. Our teacher had a knife stuck to her forehead and a spoon dangling from one ear. When we got back to our table, the party at the next table asked, "Do you folks come here often?" One of the guys asked why they wanted to know. They said, "We've had so much fun watching and listening to your group have such a great time, we want to be here the next time you come back!"

Look at all the benefits you get from laughing:

- ❖ Strengthens the Immune System
- ❖ Relieves Tension
- ❖ Eases Conflict
- ❖ Reduces Stress
- ❖ Relieves Pain
- ❖ Breaks You Free of a Bad Mood
- ❖ Relaxes Your Muscles
- ❖ Gets You in Touch With Your Joy
- ❖ Gives You a Euphoric Feeling
- ❖ Produces Endorphins 200 Times More Potent Than Morphine

What could you promise yourself to do today to add more laughs to your life?

Are you willing to do it at home and at work? If not, why not?

Once I came home from work and my youngest daughter approached me with, "Mom, would you move in with Vicky so I can have my own room?" I broke into a long string of chuckles at the absurdity of her idea. "Nice try, dear. When you support a whole house you'll deserve the privilege and privacy of your own room. And when you get it, make sure no young whippersnapper talks you out of it!"

Here's my acronym for laughter:

L — oosens You Up

A — muses

U — nburdens

G — ives You Pleasure

H — eals Hurts

T — ickles Away Your Troubles

E — nergizes You

R — elieves Tension

Comedy, as distinguished from tragedy, as a genre, concerns itself with human imperfections and exaggerates them to absurdity. Comedy puts everyone on the same playing field under the same critical lens. No one is any better than anyone else. Comedy pokes fun at bad manners, raging egos, stuffy rules, and rigid attitudes. People laugh at exaggerated movements that clowns make. They laugh at unusual facial expressions and abilities such as nose and ear wiggling, dancing eyebrows, and amazing mouth contortions. They laugh at stupidity, real and imagined. Imitation evokes laughter. People laugh when they feel superior. *The Seinfeld show* used recognition humor, pointing out small realities we normally miss, like The Soup Nazi.

Bill Cosby said that if you can find humor in anything, you can survive. Remember my oldest daughter's line, *You gotta laugh; if you don't you'll cry.* Humor is life's best medicine.

No situation is immune from a humorous take on it. Think of gallows humor and hospital humor. Humor is the only thing short of death that diffuses horror. Viktor Frankl, who survived German concentration camp confinement, said: *Humor, more than anything else in the human makeup, affords an aloofness and an ability to rise above any situation even if only for a few seconds. I would never have made it if I could not have laughed. Laughing lifted me momentarily out of this horrible situation just enough to make it . . . survivable.*

Fredreich Wilhelm Netzsche has said, "Perhaps I know why it is . . . [humans] alone who laugh; . . . [they] alone suffer so deeply that . . . [they] had to invent laughter."

One of the easiest and best ways to hone your sense of humor is to laugh with children. Make them laugh. Let them make you laugh. Children are the best teachers of physical humor. Children laugh so much more often than adults because they use their body, mind and spirits creatively. When I was caring for my neighbor's son, David, I told him when I was about his age, I loved sliding down big wooden banisters. "I know how to slide down stairs without a banister," he said. He then slid down from the second floor to the first floor on his belly, laughing all the way. Then I slid down. Then we slid down together. David's mom and I were both single parents, so we did lots of things together with the children. One day, David and I were laughing so hard in a restaurant that his mother asked us both to leave until we could calm ourselves down. We were still laughing when we passed the window where they were sitting. She just rolled her eyes. That's another of my funny photos.

By now, you may be wondering what it actually means to have a sense of humor. Here are some characteristics:

- ❖ You are easy to amuse.
- ❖ You like to hear jokes and you also tell jokes.
- ❖ You can laugh at yourself.
- ❖ You can find the humorous aspects of situations.
- ❖ You can often brighten a bad situation with humor.

Humor is standing watch over life and shining a bright light on the funny things that show up. It is often spontaneous, quick and quirky. Humor can be so fast-paced you really need to be paying attention. Laughter is literally fast-paced, coming out of your mouth at 70 miles an hour.

Former president John F. Kennedy said that *there are three things which are real: God, human folly, and laughter. The first two are beyond our comprehension, so we must do what we can with the third.*

Cultivating good humor skills allows you to play with life. Former president Gerald Ford said that *humor can help you to disagree without being disagreeable.* When someone growls and grumbles at you, ask, *Are you an endangered species or is it legal to shoot you and put you out of your misery?* When someone finishes your sentence, say, *I guess I'll leave. Since you do both parts of our conversation, I'm no longer necessary.*

Make it easy on yourself while you are a Humorist in Training (HIT). Think positive and practice only one style out of the five basic types of humor:

The Anecdote—funny stories, often real, that you can tell over and over because they are original. My father and I tended to get the giggles in church. My mother would get annoyed. One particularly giggly Sunday, my mother pinched my father so hard, he yelled, "Ouch!" It struck us so funny, we laughed for the rest of the Mass.

Irony—Truth in funny packages. You can eat anything you want as long as you don't swallow. Everything is fattening in quantity—elephants are vegetarians.

One-liners—Situational funny lines. When I was 2 my father came home from World War II and I went to church in the big cathedral for the first time. When the priest began his sermon, I boomed from the back row in my big 2-year-old voice, "Daddy, daddy, who turned the radio on?"

Exaggeration—(Chattering teeth exaggeration) I was so cold I sounded like I had a flamenco dancer in my mouth.

Understatement—My last date was so uninteresting, he was less than boring.

You're right if you're thinking wit and humor come naturally to some people. However you're foolish if you believe you can't learn to make funnies out of life. Here are some ideas to get you started:

- Get joke books and practice the kind of jokes you find funny.
- Start telling jokes. If people don't laugh, recognize that, like you, they have certain favorite types of humor. One-liner fans get bored with long jokes. Others love long jokes the more contrived the better.
- Hang around funny people and imitate them.
- Look for material in cartoons, funny movies, and books.
- Add humor to your life every day. It is as good for you as the food groups, so non-fattening that it even burns calories.

If you think of laughter as mental jogging, think of humor as the jogging track. Could you run the quarter-mile track the first time you put sneakers to gravel? I remember the beginning of the running craze in the early 1980s. Suited up in new running gear, I began my short running regimen at the high school track. I should have suspected how hard it would be when I found myself alone on the track. By the time I was thirty steps into the quarter-mile circle, my whole body had mutinied. My head ached, I was holding one of my sides, and I was wheezing like an old tractor about to expire. After four days of this torture, I decided to time myself against the four-minute mile gauge. No fool, I fast-walked the mile first and it took twenty minutes. Excited, I anticipated how much faster my running time would be. You probably already guessed, it took twenty minutes. In joke parlance this is called telegraphing. No surprise, not very funny. Avoid it when telling your jokes. But remember the story while you hone your humor skills. Don't expect Bob Hope, Bill Cosby, Bette Midler, Seinfeld, Rosie O'Donnell, Robin Williams, or Whoopi Goldberg, at least not for the first decade. Anticipate that you'll get better.

Here's what you need to pack into your Humorist's Tool Box:

- One Large Imagination
- Creativity
- Sharp Silly Instinct
- Bag of Tricks
- Spontaneous Paint Brush
- A Target

Here are some tricks and techniques to increase your chances of getting laughs:

Prepare—Each funny story has three parts: set up, anticipation, and punch line. Tip: If the set up is too long, people get bored.

Practice Before Performance—Would you climb into an 18-wheeler tractor trailer and expect to back it into the loading dock slot the first time behind the wheel? Tip: Humor takes skill and skill comes from practice.

Pause Before the Punch Line—The pause is your promise to deliver a payoff to someone for listening.

Pause After the Punch Line—Give your listener time to get the joke and respond. Tip: That doesn't mean laugh at your own jokes which is in poor taste.

Prey on the Unsuspecting—Surprise people. Pull the rug out from under their expectations. *Did you put the cat out? No it wasn't on fire.*

Create Play-on-Words Humor—Put your own twist on familiar cliches, song titles, commercials and ad slogans. Surprise people with double entendres. You visit a friend during dinner. The friend asks, *Will you join us?* You answer, *Why, are you coming apart?*

Pack a Wallop into Your Punch Lines—Make them strong, short and surprising. You are an overnight guest and your hostess asks if you slept good. You answer, *No. I made a few mistakes.*

Put together Parallel, Paired Phrases—Optimists look at life through rose-colored glasses, and pessimists look through woes-colored glasses.

Pronounce Numbers in the Longest Way Possible—Twenty-seven is funnier than twenty. One thousand eight hundred is funnier than eighteen hundred. Exact numbers sound more believable than estimates and round numbers sound like estimates, one hundred people vs. eighty-one.

In the sum total of lives, the best memories to share are the funny ones, so create lots of them. Mark Twain said that *humor is a great thing, the saving thing, after all. The minute it comes up, all our hardnesses yield, all our irritations end, resentments flit away, and a sunny spirit takes their place.*

Want a self-study training program to develop your sense of humor? Get *Health, Healing, and the Amuse System: Humor as*

Survival Training, by Paul E. McGhee. (Kendall/Hunt Publishing Company, Dubuque, Iowa, 1999) You can order directly from Dr. McGhee by calling 973-783-8383 or by visiting his web site at: HYPERLINK http://www.laughterremedy.com.

Want to go on a weekend getaway and meet hundreds of funny people from all over the world? Attend The Humor & Creativity Conference in April at the City Center in Saratoga Springs, NY. The conference is put on by The Humor Project and you can get information directly by calling 518-587-8770. The Humor Resource Room alone is worth the trip.

Here is your Harvest Summary for Chapter 5: Bear Sweet Fruit

PART THREE

Harvest—Uniting Body, Mind And Spirit

When you move toward spiritual understanding, your aim has to be clear to you.

Certainly part of spiritual awareness is a sense of the value of peace in one's life. One comes to the place of peace on the planet by an active commitment to understanding self and other people, places, and things. You come from the same energy as I come from, the same energy that pushes wheat to and fro in the fields. The more you believe in and feel the connectedness of all life, the closer you will come to know within yourself a peaceful core that no person, place or thing can disturb.

What does spirituality mean to you? For some, it means getting in touch with thoughts and feelings they can't explain logically. For others, it means connection to God and all that is holy. For others, it means full-blown enlightenment, which itself carries a whole range of definitions, one of which is "spiritually smart." Whatever aim you have as a spiritual goal, know that all manner of spirituality comes to you through struggle.

Here's what the Buddha said of spirituality: "Man's function in the universe is to awaken his original mind that has been covered over by the dust of . . . delusions of the relative world, to identify with universal consciousness through zazen [sitting meditation] and self-realization, then to live a life of selflessness, wisdom, and compassion and eventually to attain nirvana."

Chapter 6

The Peaceful Garden—All Is One

Introduction

As a human, you are a triune being, made up of body, mind and spirit, with spirit permeating all. When you mature your spirituality you move beyond your five senses. In discovering your mature spirit you come to know love, joy, and peace in their purest forms. Spirituality manifests itself in your life as an impenetrable core of inner peace. In the spiritual world you feel with your heart and imagination. Within the spiritual world hope is always everlasting.

At thirty, I began my spiritual quest in a frenzy of workshops, books, psychics, prayer, meditation, and intellectual discussion. Spiritual people are flexible; I was ramrod rigid in my ideas. Spiritual people allow; I fought everything that I didn't like. Spiritual people believe in the perfection of the universe; I knew how to change everybody and everything. Twenty-five years later I still find myself on my soapbox now and then. As a spiritual person in training, or SPIT, I continue to fight my judgmental and superior attitudes, the need to be right, the urges to gossip, the desire for status and preferential treatment, and other demands of an ego that wants to be in charge. My mother taught me in life you have to learn to take the good with the bad and to remember only the good things. This lesson was so hard for me that only recently have I been able to live it. To keep myself grounded in the spirituality I desire, every day I say this Spirituality Mission Statement that I wrote on Saturday morning, March 2, 1996:

SPIRITUALITY MISSION STATEMENT

Every day I clearly nurture my physical, mental, and spiritual selves in balance. Every day I keep my feet grounded, appreciate nature and live life with my whole self. Every day I reflect on life, do my best, be my best, love my best, give my best, and make the best choices to achieve the highest quality of life my God-given gifts allow. Every day I value my God-given free will and the free will of others and recognize the balance and the reality of interdependence. Every day I am patient with myself and others as I strive to build a legacy with my gifts to help people achieve their best selves. Every day I exercise my mind and body, feed them thoughtfully and receive from them their best. Every day I laugh, look for fun and the light side of life. Every day I use my intuition to see the truth, to find the messages in challenges, and stay on track when strong forces of my own nature, and others, make it difficult. Every day I feel gratefulness for those in my life and those I meet on my path and I accept and give abundantly.

My personal spiritual journey has brought me to a place where three global beliefs guide my life:

- ❖ There exists a Power greater than I.
- ❖ Love is all there is that is important to be given or gotten in this life.

- ❖ All is one, making me connected with every one and everything that exists in the world along with the Power that is greater than I.

Within the context of there is one way to goodness, the spiritual journey, and many paths to evil, the spiritual journey is an interior life filled with love, joy, and inner peace. A spiritual life is a life of contemplation and good works. The purpose of the spiritual life is to serve and by serving in a personally unique way make a positive difference in the world.

Peace Pilgrim said that *to find inner peace, or happiness, you must go through the spiritual growing up. You must leave the self-centered life and enter the God-centered life—the life in which you see yourself as part of the whole and work for the good of the whole. When you have found inner peace, you are in control with the source of universal energy and cannot be tired.*

Peace Pilgrim was born in 1909 in Egg Harbor, New Jersey, of German parents with the given name Mildred Norman. In 1953 when Peace Pilgrim was forty-four years old, the bombing of Hiroshima had festered in her heart, mind, and spirit. During that time Mildred Norman became the first woman to walk the length of the Appalachian Trail. During that journey she gained inner peace and never fell backward as she had other times. At the end of the Trail she had a profound spiritual experience and saw a vision of her pilgrimage. She felt called to bring a message of peace to the world. She changed her name, sold all she had, and made a pact with God that if God would keep her healthy, she would trust in God's Divine Providence on her quest to bring her message of peace to the world. Of her pilgrimage, Peace Pilgrim said, *I am a pilgrim, a wanderer. I shall remain a wanderer until mankind has learned the way of peace, walking until I am given shelter and fasting until I am given food.*

With the clothes on her back, she began her walk for peace. In the first eleven years, Peace Pilgrim walked 25,000 miles through the United States, Canada, and parts of Mexico. She carried no money, had no possessions except a comb, a folding toothbrush, a map of the area, and her forwarded mail, which she would answer when provided a place to stay. She slept where invited and ate what was offered or she slept beside the road or in a haystack and fasted. When no shelter was provided she washed herself and her clothes in streams. Peace Pilgrim always insisted *if I can gain inner peace you can, too.*

Since Peace Pilgrim died in 1981, the Cold War ended when Russia abandoned communism, the Berlin Wall came down uniting Germany, and after twenty-nine years of persecution, Cuba Christians convinced Castro he was wrong when he declared Cuba an atheist country. I have hanging on my office wall a photograph of a mural of the Sacred Heart of Jesus that is several stories high mounted on a building in Havana's Square of Revolution where Pope John Paul II said Mass. In 1998, Cuba openly celebrated Christmas for the first time in decades.

Peace Pilgrim's message is carried on today by Friends of Peace Pilgrim out of a two-bedroom home where materials are mailed free to 100 countries all over the world. Donations are accepted but never solicited. If you feel drawn to her message, ask for Peace Pilgrim's book, *Her Life and Work in Her Own Words* at your library or book seller, or call 909-927-7678.

Search as I might, there appears to be no exact definition of spirituality, while a tie to goodness is implied. Once confined to God and holiness, mostly meaning a religious life of inner prayer, spirituality is fast becoming a mainstream term. Now, spirituality can mean a life commitment or a mere moment of joy or love or peace, or all three. Within this broader meaning, what once was the other side of the coin of materiality now draws meaning from the intellectual, emotional, and supernatural.

As we move toward the millennium, many financially successful people who have all the cars, houses, boats, planes, jewelry they could want fail to find fulfillment. Some seek to find meaning for their lives in books, seminars, workshops, and discipleship in spiritual schools. Business gurus such as Ken Blanchard (The *One-Minute Manager* series) and Stephen Covey (*Seven Habits of Highly Effective People*) speak comfortably to Fortune 500 corporations about the spiritual. The dialogue among enlightened business executives has evolved to *goodness is good business.*

The esoteric enters mainstream America from every culture, religion, mystery school, healer, and seekers such as I who want to understand how to do life in the best way possible. In 1997, adult buyers spent more than $1 billion for spiritual books, according to *R.R. Bowker's Annual Library & Book Trade Almanac.*

This renewed interest in spirituality heartens me since spirituality is inclusive rather than exclusive. Members of the various world religions are dialoging with one another. A Buddhist joke—what is the difference between Buddhists and non-Buddhists? Answer: *A non-Buddhist thinks there is a difference.* Millions wear bracelets with the letters WWJD, which asks wearers to consider what would Jesus do? What Jesus would do is always loving and accepting and forgiving. More and more people understand what it means to look for God in everyone.

Many people who want life to have a higher meaning seek a way to learn how to get in touch with their spiritual selves. I teach a nine-point personality

The Spiritual Mind Map Exercise

For those of you who have never created a Mind Map, it is a technique to take you into your subconscious mind. As you read earlier, your subconscious mind is where all your information is stored. You complete Mind Maps to reveal your personal life history about a subject. I'd like you to create a Mind Map on spirituality. Please suspend your disbelief and humor me for this exercise. This last chapter will mean so much more to you when you begin it with your innermost thoughts on spirituality.

You create your Mind Map by taking a clean 8-1/2 x 11-inch sheet of paper and smooth-writing pen or pencil. Turn the paper in the horizontal or landscape position. Draw an oval in the center of the page and write the word Spirituality in the center of the oval. You make the Mind Map by

drawing lines out from the oval and writing a new word or thought at the end of each line. The Mind Map ends up looking like a sun with words at the ends of each of its rays.

Take three deep belly breaths in through your nose and out through your mouth. Breathe in to the thought "I am connected" and breathe out to the thought "All is one." Set a timer to ring after three minutes. Your goal is to spontaneously write as many words or thoughts at the ends of the lines you draw as fast as you can. Avoid thinking about what comes into your mind. You want to produce as many different words or thoughts about spirituality as possible.

system to help people gain inner peace by getting in touch with their spirituality, or higher self. My system is called Character Architectural Technology℠ (CAT) and uses the Enneagram, a dynamic system that evolved out of oral tradition that helps students understand how their human nature works and shows them a path to their divine nature, or spirituality. Each of the system's nine personalities has a distinct human nature and a different path to connect with their divine nature. The basic CAT system is the subject of an upcoming book.

When you look at Peace Pilgrim as an example of a spiritual person, you may wonder where that leaves you. Perhaps more like me than Peace Pilgrim. The way of spirituality is different for each person. Peace Pilgrim dedicated her whole life and walked for peace, while I, like so many others, do what I can.

I liken the spiritual life to jumping into a sea of goodness where unconditional love and its possibilities are vast.

How do you begin? What is the right way for you? Intuition opens the door to spirituality. Meditation opens the door to spirituality. Prayers open the door to spirituality. Love opens the door to spirituality. Music and art open the door to spirituality. Breath opens the door to spirituality. For Camille Giraldi of The Possible Dream Foundation in North Carolina, love for children and adults with Down's Syndrome opened the door to spirituality. She and her husband have taken in 39 with this affliction.

Do you wonder why you need to get in touch with your spirit and mentally plant your seed of spirituality? Your spiritual realm is the only place where you can harvest the beauty and wonder life offers.

You know you are more than your physical body because, unlike animals, you can reason. So you already know you are a body and mind being. You can choose to go from body and mind being to completion by embracing your spirit self. Helping you consider making that choice is the purpose of this chapter.

When I did this Spirituality Mind Map Exercise, I produced a thirty-six line Mind Map:

- ❖ Authenticity
- ❖ Beautiful
- ❖ Connected (to all)
- ❖ Cosmic Consciousness
- ❖ Discernment
- ❖ Divine
- ❖ Enlightenment
- ❖ Faith
- ❖ (Gentle) Goodness (in Everything)
- ❖ (Selfless) Giving
- ❖ God
- ❖ Grace
- ❖ (An Attitude of) Gratitude
- ❖ Heaven
- ❖ Holy

- (Unending) Hope
- Imagination
- Innocence
- Joy
- Laughter
- Life-giving
- Light
- (Unconditional) Love
- (Reaches Out with) Love
- (Universal) Love
- (Lovingly) Nurturing
- (Inner) Peace
- Prayer
- Responsibility
- Soul
- Strong
- Trusting
- Truth
- Understanding
- (Healthy, Moral) Virtues
- Wisdom

Before I discovered my spiritual side, I felt like an empty house. People would come and visit and sometimes fill me temporarily. Other times I could feel lonely with one or more others. As my spirituality matured, my house felt less and less empty until there came the day when I found my spiritual center, the inner peace within that nothing and no one could disturb. Now, I no longer look for someone or something to fill me up. I am body-mind-spirit complete.

The generosity of spirituality can be difficult to practice. Spiritual people understand that everybody does the best they can with what they have to work with at the time, so they take nothing personally and rarely get angry. Even if what they get from another is downright pitiful, it's okay and accepted by an evolved spiritual person. SPIT's like me still struggle with this.

Along the way realizations during contemplation are heartening. On March 9, 1996, I realized hate was not an emotion I could feel against human beings. I was reading the Norman Vincent Peale interview in William Elliott's book, *Tying Rocks to Clouds.* Dr. Peale spoke about Jesus' philosophy of love. Peale said there were no bad people, only good people acting badly.

No matter what terrible things people did, hate never came into my heart. That doesn't mean I couldn't get up a fierce dislike of what someone did. There could be tremendous anger that would rise up. Perhaps my anger gets so hot it burns away all the pain. I have flash anger that builds, blows, and gets over quickly. After I cool down, if what people did is so terrible I can't reconcile it, I let them go emotionally. After the letting go, what they did can't hurt me any more and they cease to exist for me emotionally.

By actively engaging in growing spiritually, you add dimensions that will enrich your life beyond imagination. I ask you to open yourself to your spiritual nature so you have a place to plant the seeds of your dreams so they can take root.

Dr. Wayne W. Dyer said that *you're not a human being having a spiritual experience, you're a spiritual being having a human experience.*

In defining spirit, I see spirit as an energy force that courses through each individual, functioning as living cells of a person's connection to all there is. Human beings seeking spirituality take the time to get in touch with their spirits so that spirituality can operate within them as their grounding anchor.

You may be wondering about the connection between spirituality and religion. Religious dogma is sometimes judgmental and exclusive while spirituality remains ever nonjudgmental and inclusive. The truth be told, religious people may not necessarily be spiritual and spiritual people are not necessarily religious. For me religion formed my bridge to the spiritual. The contemplative core of religion is in itself a spiritual science. My experience says, however, more spiritual people are religious than religious people are spiritual. If that sounds judgmental, consider I'm still a SPIT.

The contemplative core of both religion and spirituality poses life-guiding questions. Religion tends to answer these questions:

- Why did God make you?
- What can you do to live the right way?
- How do you pray?
- What happens after you die?

Gandhi said that like the bee gathering honey from the different flowers, the wise person accepts the essence of the different scriptures and sees only the good in all religions.

Spirituality tends to have you ask yourself these questions:

- What is the truth?
- How can I selflessly love others?
- Will this action foster peace?
- How can I use my gifts to make a positive difference in the world?

Here are eighteen characteristics of spiritual people:

- Radiate Joy
- Accomplish Change Through Uncritical Observation
- Have a Profound Hope in the Eventual Prevailing of the Good of Humankind to Triumph over Evil
- Never Appear in a Hurry
- Vow to Do No Harm

- ❖ Live in the Present Moment
- ❖ Have Boundless Energy
- ❖ Speak from a Quiet Inner Knowing
- ❖ Love All People as if They Have Never Been Hurt
- ❖ Free of Addictions
- ❖ Positive Thinkers
- ❖ Nonjudgmental
- ❖ Engage in Purposeful Action
- ❖ Have a Calm and Peaceful Manner
- ❖ Exhibit Confident Humility
- ❖ Show Compassion and Kindness
- ❖ Exhibit a Wise Maturity
- ❖ Make a Commitment to Behave Nonviolently

You may wonder how you can come to know your spirituality. Begin by recognizing that you have three ways of knowing:

Critical Knowledge—With this knowledge you think things through and reason things out, comparing, contrasting, and creating new seeds of thought.

Instinctual Knowledge—With this knowledge you assess your mental and physical environment to determine what may help you and what may hurt you.

Intuitive Knowledge—With this knowledge you move beyond the five senses, into the sixth sense that knows beyond space and time and is the door to spirituality.

Illusions author Richard Bach said that *we are led through our lifetimes by the inner learning creature, the playful spiritual being that is our real self.*

Like body, mind, and spirit the ideal is for the three to work together in balance, creating a hybrid. Intuition is outside-of-the-self

The Fear Exercise

The book A Course in Miracles *states, "I can choose peace instead of this. If you know Who will be beside you at all times on this path, you would never experience fear and doubt again."*

Because of their special freedom of choice, spiritual people have an indestructible hope. Former Czechoslovakian president Vaclav Havel said, "Hope is not the conviction that something will turn out well but the certainty that something makes sense regardless of how it turns out."

Imagine the power of letting go of outcomes and the fears that are associated with gloom and doom possibilities.

sense that some call *uncommon sense*. Intuitive knowledge raises possibilities and critical knowledge determines how, while instinctual knowledge watches your back. Spiritual knowing is evolved intuition.

Persian Poet Rumi said that *out beyond all ideas of right and wrong there is a field. I'll meet you there.*

The way of the spiritual person is the peaceful way. To know inner peace is to lack for nothing and feel no fear. With inner peace comes a security that allows you to meet the good and the evil in life in peace.

Imagine no fear, only peace. Consider that you never really fear what is currently happening, since there is no fear in the present. A popular acronym for fear is False Evidence Appearing Real. Fear is a projection of a future you don't want to happen. You were born without fear. That's why as a baby you had to be watched so closely. You learned every fear you have. Your fear takes you to aggressive fight or flight response or to low energy withdrawal response. So the fears you imagine either pump you up or wear you down, depending on your natural automatic response inclination.

I remember as a child, walking with my mother, my aunt, and my three-and-a-half-year-old cousin. Johnny bolted away from his mother into the street and got hit by a car. His mother in low energy withdrawal froze. My mother picked up Johnny who was stunned but not hurt.

Only a few highly evolved spiritual beings can conquer all their fears as Peace Pilgrim did. These three strategies, however, can help you fight your fear responses:

Focus Your Attention in the Present—This stops your horror movies of the future you don't want to happen and allows you to take present moment action.

Control Negative Mental Static—If you let them, your worry, negative what-if scenarios, and fear projections will control your thoughts. Worry is interest paid on trouble before its due. Negative programming fogs your mental clarity and saps your energy. Fear paralyzes you. Belly breathe your way through bad thoughts. Banish them by intentionally taking deep breaths where you breathe in positive thoughts and breathe out the negative ones.

Face Your Fears—Sit quietly and go into the fear projecting it to the absolute worst thing that could happen. Look at that dire consequence and examine it. Consider how much control you have over it happening. Look at positive action you could take. Feel the fear and then watch it disappear. Fear is an emotional bully. Stand up to it with your faith and it almost always backs right down.

So many stay stuck in bad relationships. They are like stupid Asian monkeys trappers catch because they refuse to let go of the fruit trappers place in small holes in gourds that they tie to the ground. The fist the monkeys form gripping the fruit traps their hands inside the gourds. So the monkeys actually trap themselves neither able to enjoy the fruit they hunger for nor escape. Doesn't that sound a lot like the description of bad relationships?

I once met a man who stunned me when I saw him. He looked just like the prince on my childhood *Cinderella* Little Golden Book. Like Cinderella, I loved him and wanted to be his princess. It was not to be, because he didn't see me as his princess. For years I thought of him. Then I went through a consciously angry period where I wanted to punish him. Then I just wanted so much to forget him and get on with my life. Years passed and I stayed in that stuck place. Until I came to understand that forgiveness would heal me, he cluttered my mind and kept my heart closed. Once I could give up the belief that he deserved to suffer, I could let go of my hurt and anger and move on. All those years after the relationship ended, I suffered until I could forgive, heal, and learn a valuable life lesson: Walk through the doors that open.

Now when people ask me why I am not married, I tell them I am like Nasrudin who, in his youth, searched the world over for the perfect woman to marry. When he found her, he could not marry her—she, you see, was looking for the perfect man!

Other people stay stuck in feelings of what they lack keeping their minds ever in a frenzy of madness for more. What is lack? To want is to feel deprived. Instead of feeling fulfilled by what they do have, the lackers lust after what they do not have. With their minds focused on scarcity they feel no satisfaction.

Dr. Wayne Dyer said that anything you must have comes to own you. Ironically when you release it, you start getting more of it.

Spiritual people practice the Buddhist concept of non-attachment. No material thing rules them, not money, not trappings, not toys. Non-materialistic spirituality is all encompassing, like a compass that always leads you in the right direction on your path of evolution.

You may be wondering how you know you are on your right path. Recognize first that it's a far different life when you struggle to keep your flame burning than it is when you challenge yourself to make your flame give more heat. John Powell, S.J., said, *There is an old Christian tradition that God sends each person into this world with a special message to deliver, with a special song to sing for others, with a special act of love to bestow. No one else can speak my message or sing my song or offer my act of love. These have been entrusted only to me.*

When you come to do your right work, your divine work, you feel its rightness in your body, mind, and spirit. Simply, when you do right it feels right. When your conscience nags at you it is because what you did doesn't feel right to your spirit. When you perform service that benefits the planet, you feel useful. When you give love and receive love, you feel connected and know happiness. But only when you feel a part of a whole greater than yourself do you feel inner peace.

Mother Teresa said that *the Fruit of Silence is Prayer; the Fruit of Prayer is Faith; the Fruit of Faith is Love; the Fruit of Love is Service; the Fruit of Service is Peace.*

You may be thinking that joy is missing from Mother Teresa's contemplative journey to inner peace. Joy comes before the journey. For Mother Teresa, first a novice has to have joy in her heart before she can become a Sister of Charity. If you do not have joy yourself, what can you bring to life, to love, to others?

Emotional maturity brings with it a capacity to feel joy and, therefore, an ability to give and receive happiness. Happy people feel enthusiastic and excited about life. They feel joyful and secure with an unshakable core of inner peace.

The Self-Forgiveness Exercise

What bothers your conscience weighs you down mentally, emotionally, and spiritually. In this exercise you look at your guilty memories of things you've done or failed to do that you regret to this day. Write down each one. When you are finished write yourself a To Do List of how you plan to right each act or failure to act you still feel was wrong.

Here's an example out of my conscience. Money was scarce with two young children. The only thing I had left from an abundant life was my collection of coats. One day my husband asked me and I gave someone special to him my ski jacket. Soon afterward he asked me to give her sister one of my three winter coats. When she tried on my red wraparound coat, it looked beautiful on her. At the last minute, I just couldn't give it up. For me my coats allowed me to deny my poverty and lack of hope in the future. After that night, I could also never wear the coat again. My most selfish act bothered me for years until I started giving away coats and jackets. This year, so far, I've given away nine.

You may be wondering where the ego fits into this formula for inner peace. Out of control, the ego seeks instant gratification in its wants and demands. The spiritual person is infinitely patient. Rather than pushing for anything, embracing the spiritual life allows all things. That is the remarkable difference.

Spirituality seeks only to build never destroy. Rather than death to the ego, spirituality brings the ego into optimum function. Within the ego lies your self-esteem, the part of your personality that believes in your ability to do.

Mahatma Gandhi once wrote that there were seven sins in the world: Wealth without work, pleasure without conscience, knowledge without character, commerce without morality, science without humanity, worship without sacrifice, and politics without principle.

You are about to reach an exciting part of the book but first I'd like you to prepare your heart. The heart of a spiritual person loves as if it has never been hurt. You've been hurt. You've hurt others, either knowingly or unknowingly. When you forgive those who have hurt you, you free yourself for happiness and spiritual growth. When you hold onto hurt you really want the person to suffer equal punishment for your hurt or at least apologize for it.

How blessed are they who have learned to forgive without remembering and who receive forgiveness without forgetting.

When you accept others as they are in the moment you stop planting new seeds of hurt and anger. When you forgive yourself you send your subconscious a message that you deserve happiness.

Lessons about forgiveness are hard learned. True forgiveness is a difficult plant to bring to harvest. Egos tend to get in the way and produce flawed forgiveness:

- ❖ The flaw of saying you forgive while hoping the other person will change or apologize. (The flaw that kept me stuck over an ended relationship.)
- ❖ The flaw of using forgiveness as a way to stay in a co-dependent cycle where repeated bad behaviors are allowed and forgiven.
- ❖ The flaw of thinking you are superior to others because you have forgiven them.

David Augsburger said that *since nothing we intend is ever faultless, and nothing we attempt ever without error, and nothing we achieve without some measure of finitude and fallibility we call humanness, we are saved by forgiveness.*

If you look at harboring past hurts as huge boulders on your spiritual path, you see that you forgive to heal yourself not others. You repent your bad deeds and ask forgiveness to heal yourself, as well. Your life is about you, not about others.

Carlos Castaneda wrote in *The Teachings of Don Juan, Any path is only a path, and there is no affront to oneself or to others in dropping it if that is what your heart tells you . . . Look at every path closely and deliberately. Try it as many times as you think necessary. Then ask yourself, and yourself alone, one question . . . Does this path have a heart? If it does the path is good; it if does not it is of no use.*

When you reach spiritual maturity you will have no need to forgive for you will have moved beyond blame. You will also make more discerning choices so you will need to ask for forgiveness less often.

You are now at the exciting place I mentioned earlier. For readers who chose this book for its title or readers who want an expanded spiritual life, or both, it's time to plant your seed to grow your spiritual life.

Wayne Dyer writing in *Manifest Your Destiny* reads, *Your desires, cultivated as seeds of potential on the path of spiritual awareness, can blossom in the form of freedom to have those desires in peace and harmony with your world.*

At some point the person who feels fulfilled planted the seed of spirituality within. That spiritual seed once planted connects the fulfilled person to all that is. As the spiritual seed roots and grows one comes to knowingly understand all is one.

All is one means that all the people who have ever lived and all the knowledge they ever knew exists as an energy. You are part of that energy and planting your seed of spirituality gives you the awareness of your connection to all that is, ever was, and will be. I call this knowledge Cosmic Consciousness. I have also heard it called God-Consciousness, Universal Consciousness, Enlightenment, Akashic Records, and Universal Knowledge. From the most elementary awareness of this knowledge babies suckle, animals hunt for food, and creatures survive.

Of course you want to access it all now. How exciting to get in touch with Galileo, Michaelangelo, Einstein, Pavlov, Joan of Arc, Jesus, Buddha, Mohammed, Solomon, Abraham Lincoln, Edgar Cayce, and Rumi. Allow what comes. In the quiet emptiness of your mind, wisdom will come. How much? Enough. How often? Often enough. Your spirituality remains in a constant state of evolving. Remember a sign of spiritual evolution is infinite patience.

Here are some instructions for seeking spirituality and union with your Higher Power from St. John of the Cross:

To reach satisfaction in all
desire its possession in nothing.

To come to possess all
desire the possession of nothing.

To arrive at being all
desire to be nothing.

To come to the knowledge of all
desire the knowledge of nothing.

To come to the pleasure you have not
you must go by a way in which you enjoy not.

To come to the knowledge you have not
you must go by a way in which you know not.

To come to the possession you have not
you must go by a way in which you possess not.

To come to be what you are not
you must go by a way in which you are not.

—(*Ascent of Mount Carmel in The Collected Works of St. John of the Cross*, Trans. Kavanaugh and Rodriguez, Washington, DC: Institute of Carmelite Studies, 1973, Book I, Chap. 13, No. 11.)

When you walk the earth as a spiritual person you are a beautiful fountain from which others may drink. Your spiritual evolution in full bloom will yield you a rich, lush and full life.

When you feel the moment is right, go inside and plant our seed of spirituality in your heart and begin growing yourself a life you'll love. For those of you who are SPIT's like me, go inside and send love to your spirit and express gratitude for its role in your life.

I wish you joy on your journey and confident humility in the miracles that befall you. Write to me about your miracles, care of Thomas More Publishing, 200 East Bethany Drive, Allen, Texas 75002.

Here's a poem I wrote for you called S O A R:

FLY
Feel Air
Breathe the wind
Float as a feather

BE
Just you
Without your cover
Open to the world

TRUST
Worthy soul
See the love
Take on your quest

SOAR
Find wings
Make them fly
Let them take you

Here is your Harvest Summary for Chapter 6: The Peaceful Garden–All is One

APPENDIX

HARVEST SUMMARIES FOR CHAPTER ONE: BELIEFS THAT ROOTBIND, LIMITING GROWTH

1. Secrets and Lies Section, p. 19
   - A. Four Main Points:
     1. Expose your secrets and lies as the relationship killers they are.
     2. Your biases determine your attitudes, which determine your feelings, which drive your actions.
     3. When you choose to live in the present moment, change is possible, and positive change grows you a life you'll love living.
     4. Yesterday is fruit eaten, a bloom spent; tomorrow is only a possibility; and today, only today, is in full bloom—so pick and enjoy today's fruits and blossoms.
   - B. Water and Fertilize New Growth By:
     1. Keeping up the detective work you started on secrets and lies by adding to your sheets.
     2. Keeping up the detective work you started on your many faces by adding to your list.
     3. Keep working on present moment focus and avoid getting stuck in yesterday or tomorrow.
2. Assumptions and Presumptions Section, p. 30
   - A. Three Main Points
     1. Avoid assuming the right to make up in your head what thoughts are in the heads and what feelings are in the hearts of other people.

2. Use a camcorder approach in your interactions with people and ask what people are thinking and feeling, listening with 100 percent of your attention to what they are willing to tell you.
3. Practice good conversational listening skills and be willing to do the hard work of attentive listening.

B. Water and Fertilize New Growth By:

1. Keep finding and examining your generic labels like those in the assumptions and presumptions exercise.
2. Spend a day in 100 percent camcorder mode, assuming nothing you can't see or hear.
3. Start and keep a list of every time you hear people say something about their perception of the way you are.

Harvest Summary Chapter Two: Drought – Emotions that Harden Hearts

Harvest Summary Chapter Three: Self Is Seed for the Life You Lead

Harvest Summary Chapter Four: Live and Let Live

HARVEST SUMMARY CHAPTER FIVE: BEAR SWEET FRUIT

HARVEST SUMMARY CHAPTER SIX: THE PEACEFUL GARDEN – ALL IS ONE

Barbara Garro welcomes your comments, stories, ideas and questions. You can write to her:

c/o Thomas More
200 E. Bethany Drive
Allen, TX 75002

Please enclose a stamped, self-addressed envelope.

Or . . .

Visit her website at www.ElectricEnvisions.com for an exciting journey into ways you can *"Grow Yourself a Life You'll Love."*

About the Author

Barbara Garro, MA, author, personal growth coach and workshop leader, business writer and poet, was born in Camden, N.J., in 1943. She studied at the Philadelphia Art Museum from 1963-'64. She holds a master of arts degree from State University of New York, Empire State College, Saratoga Springs, N.Y. She is currently president and CEO of Electric Envisions Inc., a company devoted to helping people stay motivated.

What made Garro write this book? "The seed for *Grow Yourself a Life You'll Love* was planted when I realized two pivotal concepts: 1) Love is all there is, and 2) The choices I make create my life."

Garro belongs to the International Coaching Federation, CPCU Society, International Enneagram Association, International Women's Writing Guild, Institute of Noetic Sciences, Academy of American Poets and Association for Psychological Type. In her leisure time, she tells stories and teaches religious education to children, paints in watercolor, enjoys travel and the outdoors and is an avid reader.

"An easy-to-read book that will gently motivate you to make the best of your life. The author shares her own personal challenges to inspire you to take action now, then provides you with simple, yet powerful, exercises you can use to '*Grow Yourself A Life You'll Love.*'"

JIM DONOVAN
Author of *This Is Your Life, Not a Dress Rehearsal*

"*Grow Yourself A Life You'll Love* is creative and unique from others I've read. This enlightening book offers us a particular way for self-discovery, personal growth and spiritual development. I guarantee you will come away knowing yourself better and understanding others in a new way."

DOROTHY K. EDERER
Author of *Colors of the Spirit*

" . . . a practical, insightful book. The exercises will free your self for new joy."

"Garro's easy, friendly writing style makes the information so simple to digest."

"Why pay huge therapist bills when this inexpensive yet profound guide can turn you on to life's solutions?"

MARILYN ROSS
Author of *Jump Start Your Book Sales*